# NAPAVALLEY

*A carved cask at Beringer Vineyards (above).*

*Following pages:*

*Vines climb up steep mountain slopes of Newton
Vineyards in St. Helena. Hillside vineyard acreage has grown steadily
in recent years, often on the sites of 19th-century plantings.*

*Above a cabernet sauvignon vineyard, stars sweep around
Polaris in a four-hour time exposure. Passing satellites create the straight
lines, while the dotted line comes from an aircraft.*

*Summer fog burns away from pine-covered slopes of Spring
Mountain. The Pacific Ocean, 30 miles away, regularly brings cool
air inland as far as the Napa Valley.*

# NAPAVALLEY

Photographs by
CHARLES O'REAR

Foreword by Bob Thompson
Text by John Thoreen

Collins Publishers San Francisco
*A Division of* HarperCollins*Publishers*

First published by Collins Publishers San Francisco,
*A Division of* HarperCollins*Publishers*

Copyright © 1990 Collins Publishers San Francisco

All photographs (unless otherwise indicated)
© 1990 Charles O'Rear.

Library of Congress Cataloging-in-Publication
Data. Main entry under title: Napa Valley
ISBN 0-00-215893-0

Library of Congress Cataloging-in-Publication Data.
O'Rear, Charles, 1941-
Napa Valley/photographs by Charles O'Rear:
foreward by Bob Thompson; text by John Thoreen.
p. cm
1. Wine and wine making—California—Napa River
Valley—Pictorial works. I. Thoreen, John. II. Title.
TP557.074   1990
641.2'2'0979414—dc20          90-2446   CIP

A Charles O'Rear Production

Printed in Hong Kong
First Printing August 1990

10   9   8   7   6   5   4   3   2   1

*Page viii:*
*An afternoon shaft of light illuminates a glass of Cabernet Sauvignon.*
*Dennis Johns, winemaker at St. Clement Vineyards, examines the clarity*
*of his new wine which will age for almost two years in 60-gallon*
*French oak barrels.*

# Preface

ASPECIAL KIND OF FEELING comes over me every time I return home to Napa Valley. It begins just north of Napa on my drive from the San Francisco airport. I smell the aromas of the evening breeze, I see long rays of sunlight scatter across the vineyards and I feel a crispness in the air as temperatures drop. For me, it's a powerful physical sensation—a feeling that goes straight for my soul.

Maybe I feel so strongly about the valley because I'm gone so much. I have been away more than I've been home and I've flown more than a million miles on jetliners. My assignments from *National Geographic Magazine* have taken me to our largest cities, to the inside of our highest technology, to the richest farms in America and into the poorest huts of primitive tribes. Wings have been strapped to my back, I've been lashed to dogsleds and I've floated down whitewater rapids—all to get the most expressive images. When *National Geographic* assigned me to photograph the valley in 1978 it changed my life. I took only one look and one breath and decided to make it my home. Since then I've continued to photograph here, especially during the harvest of 1989. And now I want to bring you a little closer to a place I love so very much.

CHARLES O'REAR

# Foreword

MUCH OF THE NAPA VALLEY'S WINE ends up in shimmering crystal goblets lifted from linen-covered tables by manicured hands.

All of it begins with work-thickened paws tending shaggy-barked vines in the cold mud of winter and the hot dust of summer.

No one—least of all a photographer—can ignore the natural beauty that accompanies the long refining process from new vine to old wine in Napa Valley. If the sheer rock walls of Stag's Leap do not capture some part of the heart, then oak-dotted meadows will, or pine-covered slopes, or tumbling banks of fog.

With all the beauty, it is still hands and their doings that reveal the essence of the valley. Noses are vital, too, of course, but their work is not to be seen. Get to the towns and the hands are right there along the main streets, to be sorted out for what they do, though it is easier and politer to look at their handiwork.

The Valley is small, hardly 30 miles end to end, and seldom more than two miles wide. In some places it is barely a quarter of that. And still it takes a long time to see it in detail, and to realize that one of its enduring mysteries is how it has room for all the personalities needed to grow grapes, transform them into wine, polish the rough first product, and then wait for the moment to bring it out at its mature, memorable best—and do the job in 200 different ways.

The Valley grew in two waves of unfettered optimism, the first during the 1870's and 1880's, the second precisely a century later. In both eras vintners erected monuments to their seriousness of purpose, some of them awesome, some overdone. Inglenook Vineyards' Bordeaux-like outlines, Beringer's Rhine House, Tiburcio Parrott's gingerbread mansion at Spring Mountain and the rocky mass of Greystone Cellars came with the first wave. Robert Mondavi's mission-like buildings, Sterling Vineyards' monastic aloofness, the ultra-modern Domaine Chandon, thoroughly eclectic Clos Pegase and Domaine Carneros's French transplant came with the new age.

Each of these buildings makes a visually riveting promise of a wine different from the neighbor's. So do scores of others. And yet their promises of individuality are far vaguer than those of the tiny details that surround and fill them.

Two side-by-side vineyards will be raked as smooth as sand traps at championship golf courses, but the vines in one will be spaced differently than those in the other, or trained straight up while canes in the next patch over are directed to droop. The reasons, the growers promise, can be tasted in the bottle.

In all of the cellars, barrel stacks run in laser-straight rows (neatness counts) but different coopers have burned their names into the heads, sure signs that the wines aging within will differ a tiny bit or more than that because winemakers use barrels the way chefs use sage, or dill. Scores of other choices reveal themselves in the same concrete ways.

At this point the Valley has more than 200 wineries, and more than 28,000 acres planted in vineyard. Efficiency would dictate fewer wineries and larger vineyards, but efficiency does not dictate much where wine is meant to be anything except average. Efficiency takes a modest place, well behind stubbornness, particularity, and perhaps, eccentricity. These latter qualities got this small valley to the forefront of California winemaking early in its history, and have kept it there for the length of its history to date.

Such are the charms that caused me to move to the Valley, and set me to daydreaming of home even when Manhattan or Beaune spreads out before me. The same ones brought Charles O'Rear to Napa Valley, and make him think of it when Katmandu or Jakarta are in view. Well, these charms plus woods full of mushrooms, and restaurants worth a detour, and uncrowded tennis courts, and night skies full of stars.

BOB THOMPSON

*St. Helena, California*

# Introduction

FEW WHO VISIT THE NAPA VALLEY ever forget the experience. Often they return to see more of the wineries and scenery; some come back to stay. The benign Mediterranean climate, not-too-large mountains, small towns and tidy vineyards are hard to resist. Indeed, even before the vineyards gained fame, Napa was attracting the wealthy of San Francisco to build summer homes and to vacation at the spas of Calistoga. Now the Valley draws a thoroughly international crowd for both pleasure and business.

Because of the idyllic setting and glamour of gastronomic feasts, the wine business seems to some visitors more like a game than a business. It is indeed a business, a cyclical one that knows good times and bad. Its fortunes turned downward with Prohibition, remaining that way for nearly half a century until the current upswing started twenty-five years ago. In those few years, Napa Valley has become a mix of worldly investors and down-home winemaking perfectionists who team up with young enologists, scientific vineyardists and scores of field laborers to live out their dreams.

With such newness in mind, the fame Napa Valley enjoys in the 1990's is truly amazing. And in some important ways, it is misunderstood. For example, Napa Valley is not the wine country, not quantitatively. It produces roughly 5% of California's wine, including some of the best and most newsworthy. Also, the Valley is not just now. If we look back to its early commercial winemaking, in the 1860's and 1870's, we find some interesting parallels with today: Some of its triumphs are not so new; nor are some of the challenges it faces.

At the northern end of the Valley, Dutch Henry Canyon cuts deeply into the eastern ridge and, over the millennia, has spewed an alluvial fan of rocks and gravel onto the Valley floor. Grapegrowers have twice planted this difficult bed of rocks to vineyards, first in the nineteenth century and again in the last half of the twentieth century. In a gravelly section of the present vineyard, three palm trees rise incongruously 120 feet above the vine rows. They mark the site of a home occupied in the 1870's and 1880's by Lily Hitchcock Coit, a femme célèbre from San Francisco who by age 19 had charmed Napoleon III's court during a two-year stay in Paris. Charismatic, intelligent and iconoclastic, she preferred the company of men to women. And not in idleness. When she wanted to play poker in the men's section of a St. Helena saloon, she dressed in men's clothing. Her 400-acre estate, which Lily named Larkmead, included 130 acres of vineyard in which she seemed to take a genuine interest, asking advice of her neighbors about it. Her socializing, however, got most of the attention: In a phrase of the day, "Larkmead was the hot spot of Napa Valley, and Lily was its flame."

Lily, who was financially independent, lived in the Valley during mixed times. The early 1870's had boomed, but later in the decade Napa was hit by the aftershock of an international depression and attacked by a plant louse that had already ruined the vineyards of Europe. In the 1880's, though it would not have occurred to the bourbon-loving Lily, the wine growers might have felt the heat of Carry Nation's temperance movement.

Lily's precursors and contemporaries put some extraordinary energy into building the wine business. George Yount, who built Napa Valley's first community, Yountville, planted the first vineyard in 1838 and made some wine in the mid-1840's. More serious commercial planting of vineyards started in the 1850's. Then, in 1858, Charles Krug brought a cider press from Sonoma's Buena Vista and made the first wine by modern techniques. He founded, in 1861, the winery that bears his name. Settlers seemed thirsty for northern California wine, and by 1870 there were twenty or more wineries in the Napa Valley.

The 1880's exemplify perfectly the on-again, off-again cycles of the wine business. Napa Valley inherited the plague mentioned before, phylloxera, a plant louse that spread rapidly through the soil of the vineyards, eating the roots of the vines. The vineyards needed replanting. Even though deep recession had cut down the market for wine, the replanting proceeded and turned into overplanting. There were 38 wineries in 1880, 54 in 1881 and 140 in 1888. In spite of wildly fluctuating grape prices, Napa Valley grape acreage increased. In 1881, Napa recorded 4,000 acres of wine grapes; by 1888 there were 14,000 acres. From 1890 until fateful Prohibition in 1919, the acreage hovered around 10,000 acres.

Of the many early producers, only a few survived, Krug, Beringer and Inglenook among them. In 1876, Jacob Beringer, who worked for Krug, brought his brother Frederick from Germany and started a winery across the road from Krug. In 1879, Gustave Niebaum, a wealthy Finnish fur trader, bought the property called "Inglenook" and set out to make wine as good as any in the world. Niebaum succeeded, finally winning medals in Paris in 1895.

When one talks about Prohibition, it is impossible to overstate the damage done to American taste, literal and metaphorical. It was a misguided show of zeal that created a violent and lucrative underground, put more "fun" into drinking alcohol because it was, sort of, illegal, and ruined the taste buds of America because speakeasies had no time to pay attention to the palatability of drink or food. At the turn of the century, those Americans who drank wine chose table wine, wines of moderate alcohol content. Most of this was dry (i.e., not sweet). After Prohibition, however, much of the wine was for "winos". Coarsely fabricated "Ports" and "Sherries," 20% alcohol, 10% sugar and about as sweet as cola, dominated the wine shelves.

This taste for sweet wine and the image of wine as "swill" lasted a long time. Throughout the 1940's and 1950's dessert wines counted for 75% of the wine market. Only in 1967 did table wine pull even with dessert wines in sharing the market! That marked the beginning of a new generation. Today table wine, mostly white, accounts for more than 65% of the wine in the marketplace. Wine coolers, sometimes reported as table wine, account for another 16%.

In addition to turning the American palate toward sugary wines, there was another twist of Prohibition that corrupted the vineyards of California and actually caused the acreage of wine grapes to increase during Prohibition's early years. Under the Volstead Act, the legal declaration abolishing alcohol consumption, a head of household could make 200 gallons of "non-intoxicating cider and fruit juice" for consumption at home. Of course, the fruit juice became wine, and a great demand arose for wine grapes. Long trainloads of grapes left California for Cleveland, Pittsburgh and Long Island loaded with mediocre wine grapes whose chief virtue was their ability to withstand the trip.

Not only did the wineries have to retool and revive their winemaking skills after Prohibition, they were farming thousands of acres of low quality grapes. It was, de facto, impossible to make great wine.

In 1935, the U.S. Department of Agriculture conducted a soil survey of the Napa Valley and created a colorful map outlining its 50-odd soil types. An accompanying booklet revealed that four red wine grape varieties accounted for 90% of the Valley's plantings, then about 12,000 acres: petite sirah, 40%; alicante bouschet, 25%; zinfandel, 15%, carignane, 11%.

No white grape varieties were mentioned. No cabernet sauvignon, no pinot noir. Today, few wine drinkers remember alicante bouschet, but in the 1920's it became the favorite shipping grape. Since the pulp as well as the skin of alicante bouschet carries red pigments, fermenting vats could be stretched with some water and extra sugar to more than double the production of a wine more or less red.

The rebuilding of the wine industry took many years. After dozens of quick profiteers went broke in the first two or three years after Prohibition, Napa Valley's wineries settled down to make whatever wines they could sell. A few familiar names came through Prohibition making sacramental and medicinal wines: Beaulieu Vineyard and Beringer among them. Other names appeared, Martini and Mondavi among the most influential. Still, as recently as 1960, Napa Valley

Immigrants have always played an important role in building the Napa Valley. The first winemakers and grape growers were, by definition, immigrants to California, even if they made the trek from South Carolina, as did George Yount. Other principal characters came from Northern Europe: Charles Krug, Jacob Schram and the Beringer brothers from Germany, and Inglenook's Gustave Niebaum from Finland. Georges de Latour founded Beaulieu Vineyard, bringing a French influence.

By hook and by crook these names survived Prohibition; many other winemaking pioneers, immigrants and Americans alike, did not. After Prohibition, two Italian families came to stay in the Napa Valley: the Martinis and the Mondavis. The patriarchs of each family had come from Italy. Now their children and grandchildren carry on the family businesses.

Immigration continued but on new terms. A few winemakers arrived in Napa Valley as a result of difficult wartime and political events. In the recent heyday of Napa Valley, immigrants have been investors as well as winemakers. They've come from England, Switzerland, France, Italy, Chile, Sweden and Japan. For all of Napa Valley's appearance as a part of rural California, the accents at social gatherings speak for a truly international coalition of immigrants.

Cesare Mondavi and his family (right) pose in Virginia, Minnesota: (from left) Cesare, Rosa, Peter, Mary, Helen and Robert. Today Robert heads Robert Mondavi Winery and, a few miles up Highway 29, Peter operates Charles Krug Winery. At a Charles Krug Winery groundbreaking ceremony in 1958 (above) Cesare and Rosa pose with sons Peter (left) and Robert (second from right).

In 19th-century grapegrowing and winemaking, "horsepower" and "manpower" had literal meanings. (clockwise) With the historical Summit Winery in the background, a crew poses proudly among young vines in 1893. Outside Sutter Home Winery about 1910, a six-horse team pulls casks of Zinfandel wine. At the Theo. Gier Winery (now The Hess Collection), pumps were manual and fermenters had open tops into which crushed grapes slid through a wooden chute. In a Valley vineyard, pickers stack boxes of grapes onto wagons for a journey to the winery.

wineries seemed to be headed toward extinction, their number having declined from 55 wineries in 1936 to 30.

In 1961, Joe Heitz, an enology professor and former assistant winemaker at Beaulieu Vineyard, bravely started Heitz Wine Cellars. Three years later, in the fall of 1964, two couples—Jack and Jamie Davies and Michael and Ann Stone—left a Wine and Food Society lunch at Charles Krug to explore two separate properties. That day the Davieses found Schramsberg and the Stones discovered the property that would become Sterling Vineyards. The next year, 1965, Robert Mondavi decided to leave the family operation at Charles Krug to try a new direction in Oakville. Those stirrings began the present era of Napa Valley winemaking.

Each of these new producers had something special in mind. Joe Heitz would become a specialist in Cabernet. Stone and his partner Peter Newton would not only plant cabernet and chardonnay but also a grape called merlot, then almost unheard of in California. Jack Davies was set on making a small quantity of sparkling wine by *méthode champenoise*, at that time practiced by only one other California producer.

By 1970, an eclectic group of individual entrepreneurs had founded wineries such as Spring Mountain, Chappellet, Freemark Abbey, and ZD wineries. They struck the mold for dozens and dozens of other small producers that would start up over the next twenty years.

The 1970's have been called the decade of the winemaker. It was the pubescence of great twentieth-century winemaking, and the times were fraught with the instability common to that phase of life. Young winemakers, most of them recent graduates from University of California at Davis, worked with increasing acreages of the world's best grape varieties: cabernet sauvignon, chardonnay, pinot noir and merlot among the most important. The same winemakers tried out small French oak barrels, not commonly used in earlier years, as a source of rich fragrances and flavors. Some of the new plantings produced excellent wines, even from young vines. Others showed promise but asked perhaps to be planted in different soil or with a different exposure to the elements.

The wine styles of the 1970's were not subtle. It seemed red wines were best if opaque, heavily oaked, and high in alcohol and tannin, "so they would age". Chardonnays gave new tasters a clear lesson in the scent of French oak, but too frequently the oak hid the complex aromas of the chardonnay grapes. We are now seeing that some of the heavily flavored, highly tannic red wines have aged less well than predicted.

The excesses of the 1970's were probably unavoidable: new grape varieties, enthusiastic young winemakers and an entrepreneurial attitude that worked on "more is better" all contributed to creating some "monster" wines.

Still, they showed plenty of promise, even when tasted against the best French wines. Of course, said the French, but it's not fair for Californians to taste French wines in San Francisco. In 1976, Stephen Spurrier, a young Englishman who bought and sold wines in Paris, staged a Franco-American competition in Paris with French judges. White Burgundies against California Chardonnays and red Bordeaux against California Cabernets. Napa Valley wines—Chateau Montelena Chardonnay and Stag's Leap Wine Cellars Cabernet Sauvignon took first place in both categories. Even given the vagaries that surround wine tastings, Napa Valley has never been quite the same.

Sometime in the late 1970's and early 1980's winemakers and winery owners alike gained a new level of stylistic awareness. It discredited the power approach to winemaking and favored a sense of measure. It also became clear to winemakers who had several vintages under their belts that a critical part of their wine style comes straight from the vineyard and not entirely from magic wrought in the winery.

This perception, obvious in hindsight, has launched the era of the vineyardists. For the last ten years, even at many startup wineries, the source of grapes has become increasingly important. In 1975, roughly one-third of the vineyards was controlled by wineries, the rest by independent farmers who sold grapes to wineries on a contractual basis. Today, the situation has almost reversed itself, with the wealthiest wineries scrambling to tie up the last acres of promising Napa Valley land.

Earlier we saw the discouraging acreage just after Prohibition, consisting primarily of four sturdy red grape varieties of no great winemaking potential. By 1961, things were not much better, in fact, there were only 9,300 acres, 3,000 less than in 1935. The varieties: petite sirah, 20%; zinfandel, 10%; sauvignon blanc, 10%; carignane, 9%; burgundy, 8%; napa gamay, 6%.

While one white grape, sauvignon blanc, had made inroads, there was still hardly any cabernet sauvignon (under 400 acres, 4%) or pinot noir (150 acres, 2%); chardonnay did not make the list. In the quarter century following Prohibition, the dominant Napa Valley grape varieties had hardly changed at all!

But just twenty years later in 1980, we could say there had been a revolution in the vineyards: With more than twice the acreage than in 1961, 22,000 total acres, the varieties read quite differently: cabernet sauvignon, 23%; chardonnay, 14%; pinot noir, 11%; zinfandel, 9%; napa gamay, 5%; petite sirah, 3%; sauvignon blanc, 3%; merlot, 3%.

Some of our old grape friends—alicante bouschet, carignane, burgundy—had become ghosts. And, at last, we had a significant acreage of the world's best grapes: cabernet sauvignon (with a bit of merlot), pinot noir and chardonnay. These encompassed, in terms of grape varieties, the great wines of Bordeaux and Burgundy. Strange as it is to say, only in 1980 were we prepared to start fine-tuning Napa Valley winegrowing.

Growers knew a hundred years ago that the geography of the Napa Valley—climate and soils —was the key to its success. After Prohibition, when we desperately needed to replant the vineyards, professors at University of California at Davis devised a system for measuring climates in terms of heat. They showed that Napa actually had three distinguishable heat zones, designated Region I, Region II and Region III, from coolest to warmest. The southernmost region, recently gaining fame as Carneros, is cooled by a marine intrusion, often fog, from San Francisco and San Pablo Bays. As cool as France's Burgundy, Carneros is best suited for the delicate, early ripening grapes like chardonnay and pinot noir. Further north, from Yountville to St. Helena, greater daily heat suggested that grapes like cabernet sauvignon, sauvignon blanc and merlot would do best. North of St. Helena the heat approached that of the South of France, and hearty grapes, such as zinfandel and gamay, would best take the heat.

It is remarkable that one can find the climates of Avignon and of Chablis within a 30-mile drive, but it is also an oversimplification. For the last twenty years, grape growers have been theoretically discussing microclimates, small areas that because of exposure, small ridges, special soils, altitude and other specific features offer special growing conditions. For the last ten years, growers have been defining these microclimates in practical ways. Certain areas gained official recognition from the federal government as sub-appellations of the larger "Napa Valley" appellation. Vineyards in other microclimates, even parts of vineyards, call for special farming techniques to obtain optimal grape quality. This recent focus has resulted in a growing number of single vineyard wines, Cabernets, for example, labeled "Martha's Vineyard", "Diamond Mountain Ranch", etc. We now have five sub-appellations, small sections of the Napa Valley whose names can appear officially on wine labels in addition to "Napa Valley": Carneros, Stag's Leap, Howell Mountain, Mt. Veeder and Wild Horse Valley.

The era of the winegrower will last longer than the decade of the winemaker, and it will be very costly. With land costs ranging from $30,000 to $50,000 per acre, and planting costs an additional $10,000, the investment challenges even large corporations. Moreover, it can take five years to get a full crop, and the wine made from it, if red, won't reveal its true quality for three to five more years. Most winery owners will wait longer, wanting the vines to be eight or ten years old before they feel confident about the grapes showing their best.

Thus a vineyard experiment consumes at least a decade before yielding any clear results. Since the commercial life of a vineyard is at least thirty years, the winegrower must also read the marketplace far into the future. Will there be a demand for wine made from cabernet, chardonnay, or pinot noir for the life of the vineyard?

Today Lily's Larkmead is known as "Three Palms Vineyard". Its owners, Sloan and John Upton, consider themselves tenders of Lily's ghost. They left the palms standing in her honor and believe she inspires the wine from their vineyard. The Uptons had the pluck to plant cabernet sauvignon and merlot as early as 1968. According to a leading wine magazine, Three Palms Vineyards red table wine ranks as one of the top 100 wines in the world. Lily must be a very good spirit.

We are living with another ghost from the nineteenth century—phylloxera, the plant louse that loves to eat the roots of cabernet, chardonnay and all the varieties of *Vitis vinifera*. To everyone's surprise, it has re-emerged in a new biotype, phylloxera B. One hundred years ago we escaped phylloxera by grafting vinifera vines onto phylloxera-resistant roots. Europe and other regions infected by phylloxera did the same. In the mid-1980's a few Napa grape growers discovered to their dismay that the rootstock they chose for much of the acreage in the Napa Valley is not very resistant to this revived form of phylloxera. Already growers have pulled out several hundred acres, and it is possible that most of the Napa Valley will have to be replanted over the next ten to twenty years. Perhaps we can think of this challenge as a goad to getting the vineyards into the right microclimates. This is a key part of the Napa Valley future.

By design, wine is a beverage of moderation and one used for ages to enhance the family table. About 1980, winemakers and winery owners, reacting to the powerful wine styles of the 1970's, started talking about "food wines". While we had drunk heavier wines more or less happily at table, people in the culinary renaissance pointed out that these wines accompany well only a narrow range of dishes. Wines of the 1980's, therefore, reflect a measure of subtlety, lightness and grace that we had not often tasted before. As California cuisine introduced hundreds of new, if occasionally crazy, flavors, we could also appreciate many more types of wine. To accompany these tastes, Napa Valley now produces more styles of wine than ever imagined, including a few of those hefty reds and oaky whites that some winedrinkers still enjoy. This is, after all, a vast arena for expressing personal tastes.

Along with the winemakers' insights into styling wines for food came several culinary programs developed by the wineries. Robert Mondavi has run the Great Chefs program for years, week-long schools that originally featured the best chefs of France and now of the world. Inglenook was among the first to start researching wine and food combinations and doing semi-technical demonstrations for the press and wine trade. Many smaller wineries hired chefs-in-residence. In recent years, Beringer built a Culinary Arts Center devoted to the advanced training of American chefs.

The wine and food flavors, literal and metaphorical, of the Napa Valley have never been richer. Grapes cover most of the plantable land. Wineries now number some 230, or about eight per mile, and it would take weeks to exhaust the possibilities for visiting them all. More and more frequently, visitors stay for two or three days just to visit a cross-section. A small world of restaurants shows off the wines, providing convivial, once-in-a-lifetime meals.

Happily, the idea of family, extended family, still works as a metaphor for the pulse of Napa Valley. Half of the wineries belong to the Napa Valley Vintners Association, a trade organization that determines, not always with ease, policy for winery activity and educates budding winedrinkers about vineyards and wineries. An important adjunct to the Vintners Association is the annual Napa Valley Wine Auction. In ten years it has grown to rank just behind Burgundy's Hospice de Beaune in international significance. Each June hundreds of local volunteers help to entertain 1,500 people for several days. In a huge tent at Meadowood Resort's ninth fairway, the entire group gathers for a marvelous dinner and upbeat dancing one night and reconvenes the next day for the auction itself. In its first decade the Wine Auction has raised $3.1 million for local health facilities.

Success in Napa Valley is as challenging as reconstruction. Only recently have wineries, growers, planners and local politicians been able to agree upon the definition of "winery". But because we do now understand the history, the business cycles, the pests, and exquisite fruits of our work—odds are excellent that the Napa Valley will remain a great place to visit and a marvelous home in which to live.

To your health!

John Thoreen
St. Helena, California

*"And they went out into
the fields, and gathered their vineyards,
and trod the grapes …"*

JUDGES 9:27

*A gloved worker shows off his picking knife, curved to hook the stem of a grape cluster. Cabernet sauvignon grapes (right) hang fat with sweet juice only days before harvesting at the Sorensen Ranch on the Silverado Trail.*

*Preceding pages: Pickers bring in a crop near Mont La Salle, northwest of Napa, home of the Christian Brothers since 1930. Pickers bear 40-pound boxes of grapes to a hopper, which follows the pickers through the field, staying as close as possible. Then the two-ton load may be towed as far as ten miles to be crushed at the winery.*

*A coal miner's lamp (right) lights the way for Francisco Carrillo and other pickers at Rutherford Hill and Freemark Abbey. They start work at 3:00 a.m. while the grapes are cool and less likely to oxidize on the trip to the winery. The workday for this picker ends at 9:00 a.m. Chardonnay grapes (above) picked by home winemakers wait to be pressed. Since Prohibition, Federal laws have allowed home winemakers to produce 200 gallons per year.*

*Preceding pages: A picker concentrates on cutting chardonnay grapes to fill his lug at Vine Hill Ranch near Yountville. The looping hose in front of the picker drips water directly to the base of the vines, using only a fraction of the moisture used by conventional spray irrigation.*

*Artfully balancing 40 pounds of grapes while at a steady jog, Salvador Muñoz hustles in the cool of the morning to tally as many boxes as possible before the heat of the day. Most picking is done on a piecework basis, and crew chiefs record the output of each picker.*

*Preceding pages: A crew trudges up a hill to start picking a section of a mountain vineyard. In the rough terrain, where the work is slow, the pay is sometimes hourly because workers can't earn enough at piecework rates.*

*Harvest shows many moods and many tempos. A serene young woman (above) is dressed for protection against the sun and insects. In contrast, a thirsty picker (right) cools off with a drink of water from the back of a gondola.*

*Following pages: With a hefty toss, Carmen Vega spreads pinot noir grapes into a gondola headed for the Louis M Martini winery.*

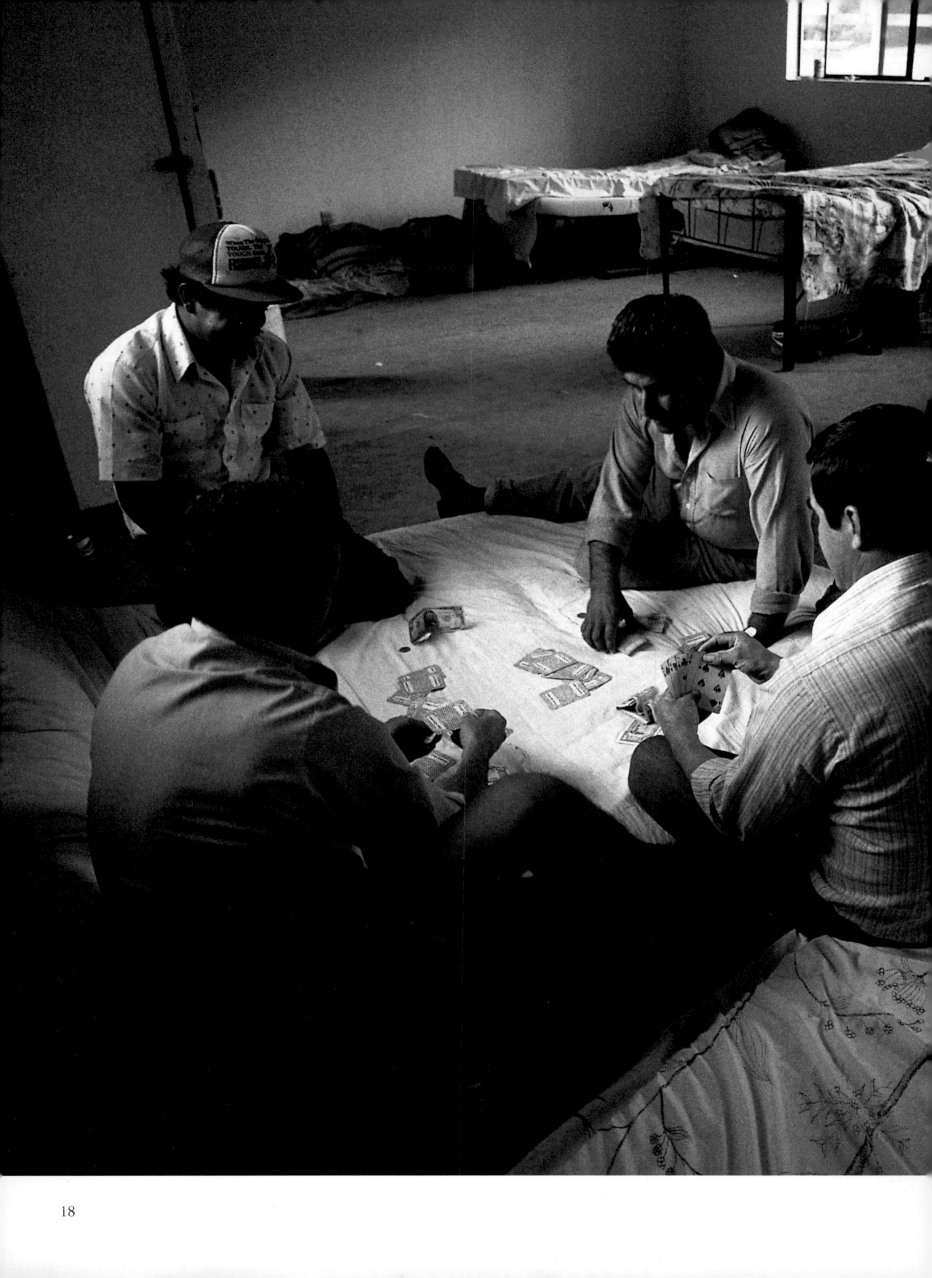

*After working ten- or twelve-hour days in the vineyards, workers take a much-needed break in a permanent dorm used during harvest season. The work force in the vineyards of the Napa Valley is predominantly Hispanic, with a core of full-time skilled farmworkers. During the harvest the number of these workers triples to keep up with the quickly ripening vineyards. The work is physically demanding and compensation reflects that fact. Year-round wages average $8 to $10 an hour, and during harvest some pickers can earn up to $200 per day. Worker Julian Leon (above) presents a strong portrait at the end of his day.*

*Jack Cakebread, who founded Cakebread Cellars in 1973, phones from the vineyards (above) to discuss where his crews will pick tomorrow. At one time a sports photographer for the National Football League, Cakebread continues to photograph professionally, specializing in agriculture and scenics. A five-ton load of chardonnay grapes from Red Barn Ranch (right) near Rutherford is ready for the slow drive to Freemark Abbey Winery, on the north side of St. Helena.*

*With early morning light as a backdrop (left), a mechanical harvester gathers grapes for sparkling wine to be made at Domaine Chandon. These vineyards near Yountville belong to the Trefethen family whose 600 acres supply grapes for their own label and for several other wineries. A box of chardonnay grapes on his head (above), a picker heads for Cakebread's portable field crusher where the grapes will be de-stemmed and crushed. The "must" (juice, skins, seeds and grape pulp) is then pumped into a tank drawn through the field.*

*Preceding pages: A mechanical harvester crests a hill in Los Carneros, southernmost region of Napa Valley. In recent years mechanical harvesting has gained steadily in approval. Now, machines harvest as much as one-fourth of Napa Valley's 28,000 acres of grapes.*

Sorting through grape clusters (left) as they arrive from the vineyard, the winery crew at Duckhorn Vineyards throws out underripe and overripe fruit, grapes that show any mildew, and MOG— "Material Other than Grapes." The cleanest fruit makes the best wine, so owner Dan Duckhorn (above) personally inspects the grapes in one of his half-ton harvesting boxes before allowing them to be crushed and fermented.

Preceding pages: Shaken from the cluster by a mechanical harvester, individual grapes, known in the trade as "berries," move up a conveyer and into a hopper near Rutherford. Stems give a bitter taste if crushed with the berries.

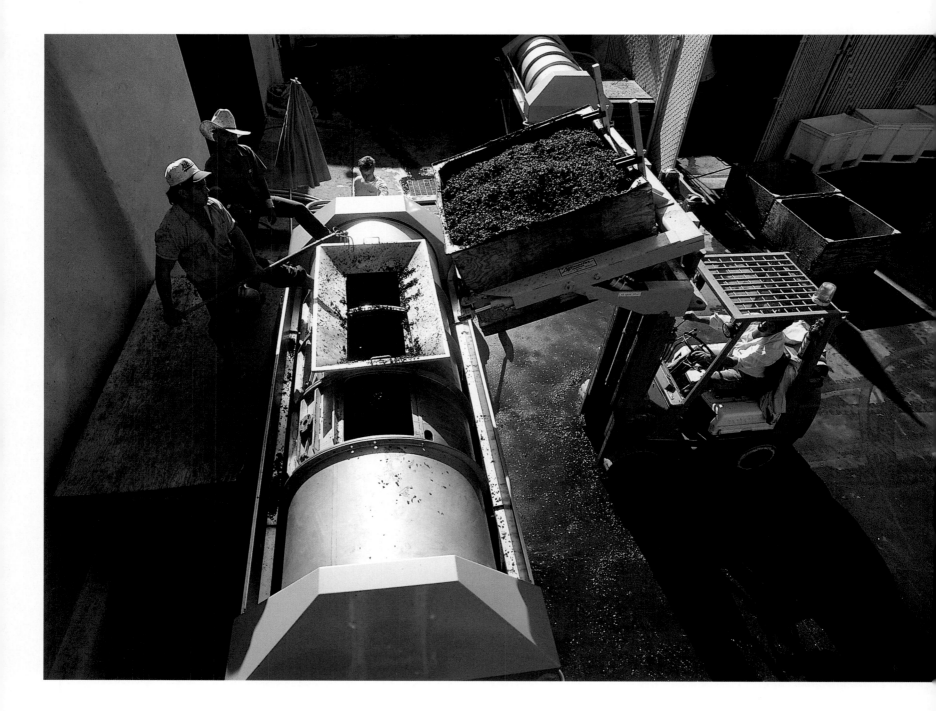

A heavy load of wooden picking boxes (left) stacks neatly on a flatbed truck. Only in recent years have lighter, cleaner, stronger fiberglass "boxes" replaced the classic wooden box. At Robert Mondavi Winery (above), cellar workers load a press with "red pomace"—the skins and pulp left after draining off "free run" wine from the fermenter. But there's still plenty of red wine left in the red pomace. Pressing will reclaim this wine, though as somewhat coarse "press wine" it might not be blended back into the premium wine.

Preceding pages: A tractor pulls three hoppers full of grapes up Diamond Mountain Road. Hoppers are pulled individually by tractors between the vine rows, and after filling they are transferred to a flatbed trailer. Later they will be pulled by a truck for faster transportation to the wineries.

Robert Pecota (above) examines the clarity of his nouveau wine. Made by a special "whole berry" (uncrushed grapes) fermentation, light red nouveau wines are drinkable just a few weeks after the harvest. Legs first, a cellar worker (right) exits crab-like from a stainless steel tank at Chappellet Vineyards. The tanks have great utility, being used for fermentation, settling, cold stabilization and storage. Between uses they are thoroughly cleaned and, if necessary, sterilized.

Preceding pages: At Mumm Napa Valley, a new sparkling wine producer owned jointly by G. H. Mumm and The Seagram Classics Wine Company, boxes of chardonnay wait to be pressed. To make delicate sparkling wines, the condition of the fruit is critical. To prevent the grapes from crushing themselves by their sheer weight, grapes are brought to the winery in small boxes instead of gondolas. Thus, reminiscent of an earlier era, this winery receives thousands of individual boxes during the six-week harvest.

Following pages: At Silverado Vineyards, Mark Del Arroyo connects a hose that will fill a fermenter with freshly pressed juice. Bands around the tanks are cooling jackets which allow the winemaker to control the temperature of fermentation. Temperature control and the length of time needed to convert grape juice into wine are only two of the factors which can affect the taste of the finished wine.

*Using a hydrometer to measure the density of fermenting chardonnay juice (above), Francoise Peschon, enologist at Stag's Leap Wine Cellars, measures how much grape sugar the yeast has converted into alcohol. At a concrete, open-topped fermenter (left) in the Louis M Martini winery, Pablo Ceja draws fermenting red wine from the bottom of the tank and splashes it over the "cap," a thick layer of skins that rises to the top of the fermenter. Since all the pigment and much of the flavors lie in the skins of the grape, this "pumping over," or some equivalent technique, is essential to making flavorful red wines.*

*At Tulocay Vineyards, owner Bill Cadman (above right) and
cellarman T. J. Schuster, set up a basket press, a classic piece of
winemaking equipment that until the 1960's did almost all the
pressing at wineries worldwide. It is still used by small wineries and
home winemakers. Schuster (right) hoses down the inside of a
stainless steel tank.*

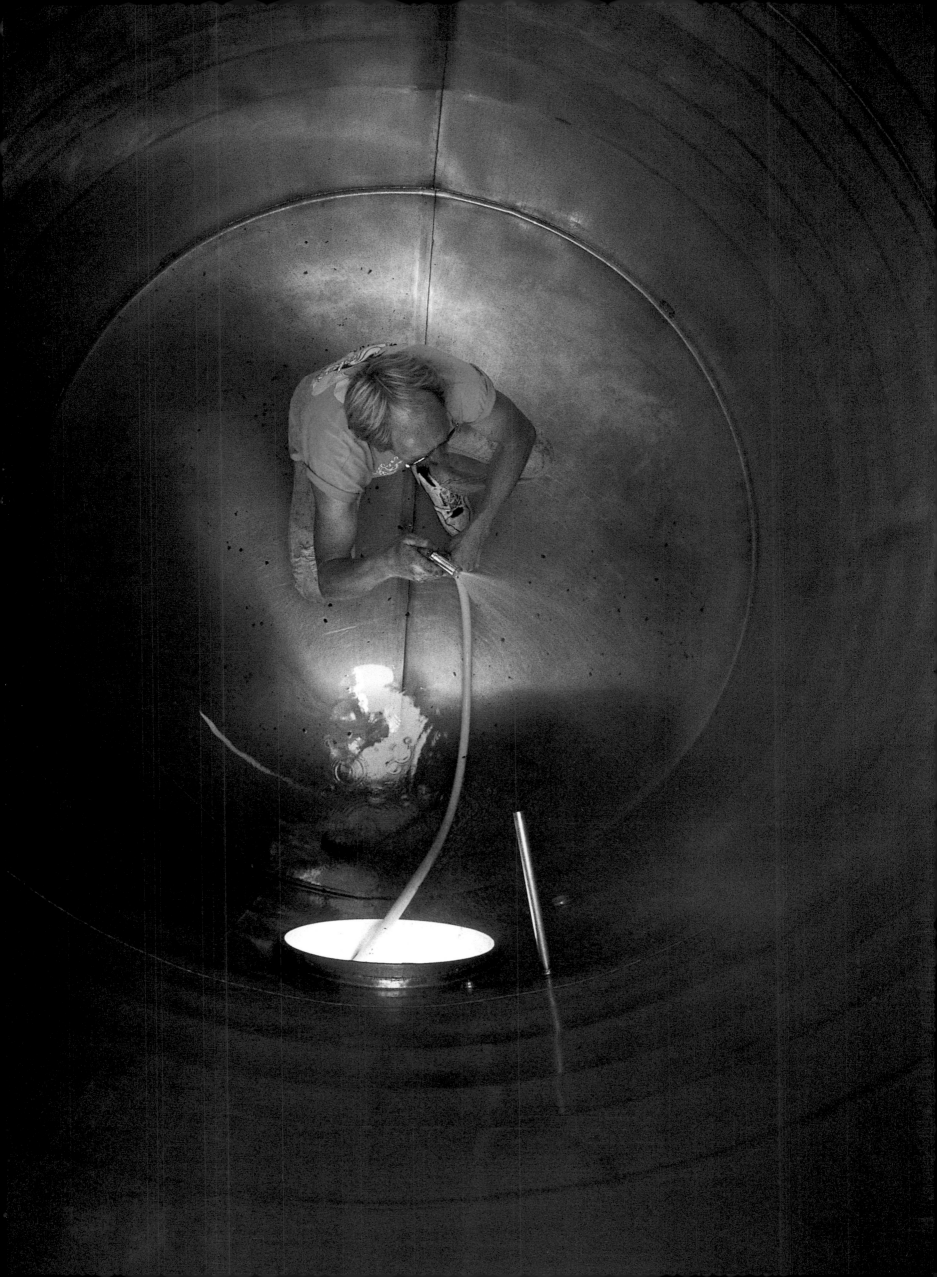

Red wine flows from a basket press. With only rare exceptions, all grapes are pressed during the winemaking process. White grapes are pressed before fermentation; in other words, grape juice flows out of the press and then goes into tanks or barrels for fermentation. For red wines, the grapes are crushed and, with their skins, put into containers for the fermentation process. During fermentation, special yeasts convert the sugar in the grape juice to alcohol in both white and red wine. After fermentation is complete, the young red wine is drained off and the left over "pomace" is pressed to collect the remaining wine. Utilizing up to 8,000 tons of stems, grape skins and seeds, which remain after the wineries have pressed their grapes (right), owner Bob Pestoni, of Upper Valley Recycling, composts it and sells it to nurseries, gardeners and grape growers as a soil enhancer. Here Pestoni checks the internal temperature of a long pile.

Paul Robinson, enologist at Louis M. Martini winery, draws new
White Zinfandel wine into a pipette to measure its acidity. Just as a
pitcher of refreshing lemonade requires the right ratio of sweetness to
tartness, the basic palatability of wine is determined by a balance
between alcohol, sugar and acidity. The gate to S. Anderson
Vineyard's caves (right) near Yountville frames winemaker Gary
Galleron as he inspects the clarity of a bottle of rosé sparkling wine.


Preceding pages: French oak barrels arrayed in rows at Chappellet
Vineyards speak for the quiet part of winemaking and also for
the capital investment required. In recent years the cost of such
barrels has soared to almost $500 apiece.

*Bottling at Louis M Martini winery (left) is straightforward and efficient. Connie Bertolucci packs bottles into 12-bottle cases. The line runs at 55 bottles per minute and has a capacity of 2,000 cases a day. High speed lines precisely fill as many as 400 bottles per minute, 14,000 cases per day, without humans touching a bottle or case. Bottling at home (above) calls for friends and patience. A hand-held filler with its simple float valve keeps the "fill level" only roughly constant.*

# Wine Labels:
# Art in the Market

WALKING DOWN THE AISLES of a wine shop can be like a stroll through an art gallery. Like so many miniatures set closely together, labels compete to be eye-catching and esthetically pleasing at the same time. While the mundane task of the label is to identify the producer and the type of wine, the label is also the focal point where wine producer meets wine buyer for a silent dialogue. The producer hopes the label will result in a sale and create a measure of loyalty to his or her brand.

Creating the image that is eventually glued to a bottle of Napa Valley wine challenges the best designers. Unlike the labels of France or Germany where history has set traditional appearances, California has no clear artistic boundaries. Most German wine labels look Gothic, Burgundian labels are dominated by flowing gold type and a horizontal line, and those from Bordeaux stand tall and often bear a line drawing of the chateau. In California, almost anything goes.

Designer Ralph Colonna, whose St. Helena-based firm has designed over 500 wine labels, explains, "Wine label design in California is personality driven. I strive to find the essence and uniqueness of people and their wine so that I can create a design that captures their style."

In this collection of 214 wine labels from the Napa Valley, you can find almost every school of design: refined images with elegant type, bold typefaces with strong blocks of color, curved and scalloped edges, intricate embossing, gold and silver foil, and at least one pentagonal shape.

As if it were not enough that labels sell wine and satisfy the egos and expectations of winery proprietors, they must also comply with the regulations of the Bureau of Alcohol, Tobacco and Firearms (BATF). BATF regulates the information that appears on labels and must approve the wording, type sizes and images on every label. Nudity, except perhaps for cherubs, is forbidden.

Occasionally, the sheer number of labels bewilders the wine drinker. There are so many brands to choose from and, after all, labels cannot be tasted. Choices are difficult. Perhaps the best advice, attributed to the late Alexis Lichine, points toward the ultimate, pleasant solution: "When deciding between wines, there is no substitute for pulling a cork."

The BATF scrutinizes the label of each wine bottle quite closely. Regulations require a *brand name* (Louis M. Martini, Acacia, Clos Pegase), and offer three options for type of wine: *varietal* (Chardonnay, Cabernet Sauvignon), *generic* (Burgundy, Chablis) and *proprietary* ("Opus One," "Insignia," "Trilogy"). *Varietal wines* must be 75% from the designated grape. If a viticultural area is named, e.g. "Napa Valley," the minimum is 85%. *Generic wines* are supposed to resemble the wines of the European region used on the label. They seldom do, though they may be decent wines. *Proprietary wines*, those with names invented by the producer, are becoming more common. They allow winemakers to discover new complexities by blending grape varieties.

To use a *vintage date* on a label, the wine must be made 95% from grapes harvested in the designated year. The bottler and the city in which the wine is bottled usually appear near the bottom of the label. The alcoholic content, with a leeway of one and one-half percent, must also appear. Regulations also require that wines containing over 10 parts per million of sulfur dioxide, a preservative, reveal that fact. Recently, government warning labels mentioning fetal alcohol syndrome, a caution about drinking and driving, and other health problems have been required on all alcoholic beverages sold in the United States.

Two additional phrases, *Estate Bottled* and *Private Reserve*, are permitted but not mandated. *Estate Bottled* means that the producer either grew the grapes on his or her land or purchased them from a vineyard over which the producer has direct viticultural control. *Private Reserve* is a term used in various ways, but wineries use it to designate a special *lot*, a specific quantity of wine that has been created with special attention or techniques. However, its meaning varies from producer to producer.

A separate back label is not required, although many wineries affix one to provide additional information such as grape variety, taste descriptions, food suggestions and winery history.

WHITEHALL LANE
CABERNET SAUVIGNON
1987 Napa Valley
PRODUCED AND BOTTLED BY WHITEHALL LANE WINERY
ST. HELENA, NAPA VALLEY, CALIFORNIA BW 4874 • ALCOHOL 13.5% BY VOL. • CONTAINS SULFITES

RESERVE
1987
Napa Valley
CHARDONNAY
ALCOHOL 13.5% BY VOLUME
PRODUCED AND BOTTLED BY
ROBERT MONDAVI WINERY
OAKVILLE, CALIFORNIA

PINE RIDGE
1986
Napa Valley
CABERNET SAUVIGNON
Estate Bottled
ALCOHOL 12.9% BY VOLUME
95% CABERNET SAUVIGNON, 5% CABERNET FRANC • CONTAINS SULFITES
GROWN, PRODUCED & ESTATE BOTTLED BY PINE RIDGE WINERY, NAPA, CA • BW 5012

1987
MARKHAM.
NAPA VALLEY
Merlot
MADE AND BOTTLED BY
MARKHAM VINEYARDS, ST. HELENA, CALIFORNIA, U.S.A.
ALCOHOL 13.5% BY VOLUME
CONTAINS SULFITES

Far Niente
NAPA VALLEY
Chardonnay
PRODUCED AND BOTTLED BY
FAR NIENTE WINERY, OAKVILLE, CALIFORNIA, USA
ALCOHOL 13.5% BY VOLUME

ESTATE BOTTLED

ALTAMURA
NAPA VALLEY    ESTATE BOTTLED
CHARDONNAY
GROWN, PRODUCED & BOTTLED BY ALTAMURA VINEYARDS &
WINERY NAPA VALLEY, CA • TABLE WINE • CONTAINS SULFITES

CALIFORNIA
SOLEIL
VINEYARDS
NAPA VALLEY
WHITE RIESLING
1986
AN OFF-DRY WHITE WINE MADE ENTIRELY FROM NAPA VALLEY WHITE RIESLING
GRAPES. PRODUCED AND BOTTLED BY CALIFORNIA SOLEIL VINEYARDS, YOUNT-
VILLE, NAPA, CALIFORNIA. ALCOHOL 10.5% BY VOLUME.

1983
J.E.Luper
Cabernet Sauvignon
NAPA VALLEY
PRODUCED AND BOTTLED BY BOUCHAINE VINEYARDS,
NAPA, CALIFORNIA • ALCOHOL 13% BY VOLUME

STAGLIN
FAMILY VINEYARD
CABERNET SAUVIGNON
NAPA VALLEY
1987
PRODUCED & BOTTLED BY STAGLIN FAMILY VINEYARD, ST. HELENA, CA  CONTAINS SULFITES  ALC. 12.9% BY VOL.

FROG'S LEAP
1987 CABERNET SAUVIGNON
NAPA VALLEY
PRODUCED & BOTTLED BY FROG'S LEAP, ST. HELENA, CA
ALCOHOL 13.5% BY VOLUME • CONTAINS SULFITES

PIÑA CELLARS
1987
NAPA VALLEY
CHARDONNAY
PRODUCED AND BOTTLED BY
PIÑA CELLARS, RUTHERFORD, CA, U.S.A.
CONTAINS SULFITES
Alcohol 13.0% By Volume

1988
SILVERADO HILL
CELLARS
NAPA VALLEY
CHARDONNAY
ESTATE BOTTLED
WINEMAKER'S TRADITIONAL METHODE
PRODUCED & BOTTLED BY SILVERADO HILL CELLARS
NAPA, CALIFORNIA • ALCOHOL 13.0% BY VOL. • CONTAINS SULFITES

KENT RASMUSSEN WINERY
CARNEROS
PINOT NOIR
1987
PRODUCED AND BOTTLED BY KENT RASMUSSEN WINERY
NAPA, CALIFORNIA, 707-252-4224
ALCOHOL 13% BY VOL. • CONTAINS SULFITES

SINSKEY
1987
PINOT NOIR
NAPA VALLEY - CARNEROS
Produced and bottled by Sinskey Vineyards
St. Helena, California, U.S.A.
Alcohol 13.0% by volume • Contains sulfites

Long
Vineyard
1987
NAPA VALLEY
CHARDONNAY
GROWN, PRODUCED, AND BOTTLED BY LONG VINEYARDS
BOX 50, ST. HELENA, CALIFORNIA. ALCOHOL 13.2% BY VOLUME
CONTAINS SULFITES

Cakebread Cellars
1984
RUTHERFORD RESERVE
NAPA VALLEY
CABERNET SAUVIGNON
PRODUCED AND BOTTLED BY CAKEBREAD CELLARS
RUTHERFORD, NAPA VALLEY, CALIFORNIA, USA.
ALCOHOL 12.5% BY VOLUME   CONTAINS SULFITES

Est. 1885
No. 25430
Of a total of 37,721 Bottles
Vittorio Sattui, founder
V. Sattui Winery
ST. HELENA, CALIFORNIA
CENTENNIAL VINTAGE
1985
PRESTON VINEYARD, NAPA VALLEY
CABERNET SAUVIGNON
CONTAINS SULFITES          PRODUCED AND BOTTLED BY
ALCOHOL 13% BY VOLUME     V. SATTUI WINERY, ST. HELENA, CA

Robert Keenan
1987
Napa Valley Merlot
Produced and Bottled by
Robert Keenan Winery, Spring Mt. St. Helena, Ca.
CONTAINS SULFITES, ALCOHOL 13% BY VOLUME

56

COLBY
VINEYARDS
1986 Chardonnay
Napa Valley
PRODUCED AND BOTTLED BY COLBY VINEYARDS
ST.-HELENA, CA. ALCOHOL 13.0% BY VOL . CONTAINS SULFITES

KATE'S VINEYARD
1988 NAPA VALLEY
CHARDONNAY
produced & bottled by Kate's Vineyard, Napa, Ca
alcohol 12.5% by volume, contains sulfites

1984
NAPA VALLEY
Sauvignon Blanc
12.5% ALCOHOL
Natural Sugar at Harvest 31% by Weight
Residual Sugar 10.1% by Weight
Estate Bottled by Macauley Vineyard, St. Helena CA
BOTRYTIS
MACAULEY

1988
L. PEREZ & SONS
GROWERS SINCE 1935
Napa Valley
Carneros
Chardonnay
PRODUCED & BOTTLED BY L. PEREZ & SONS VINEYARDS
NAPA, CA, NAPA CO., 13.0% ALC. BY VOL., CONTAINS SULFITES

THE
TERRACES
1986
NAPA VALLEY
ZINFANDEL
PRODUCED AND BOTTLED BY
W. HOGUE VINTNERS, RUTHERFORD
CALIFORNIA, ALCOHOL 12.5% BY VOLUME
CONTAINS SULFITES

GIRARD
ESTATE BOTTLED
1987
Napa Valley
Chardonnay
GROWN, PRODUCED AND BOTTLED BY GIRARD WINERY
OAKVILLE, NAPA VALLEY, CA. TABLE WINE CONTAINS SULFITES

ESTATE BOTTLED
Tudal
1986
Napa Valley
Cabernet Sauvignon
Grown, produced and bottled by Tudal Winery,
St. Helena, Ca. Alc. 13.1% by vol. Contains Sulfites

MARSTON
VINEYARD
WVV
ESTATE BOTTLED
1 9 8 4
NAPA VALLEY
CABERNET
SAUVIGNON
GROWN, PRODUCED & BOTTLED
BY. MARSTON VINEYARD
ST. HELENA, NAPA VALLEY
CALIFORNIA, USA
ALCOHOL 12.5% BY VOLUME

YVERDON
1978
NAPA
VALLEY
CABERNET SAUVIGNON
A superb, totally dry, claret-type wine aged in oak.
PRODUCED AND BOTTLED ON SPRING MOUNTAIN
BY YVERDON VINEYARDS, SAINT HELENA, CA
ALCOHOL 12% BY VOLUME

NEYERS
1985
NAPA VALLEY
CABERNET
SAUVIGNON
PRODUCED AND BOTTLED BY
NEYERS WINERY ST. HELENA, CA
ALCOHOL 13% BY VOLUME,
CONTAINS SULFITES

Graeser
1986
CABERNET SAUVIGNON
Napa Valley
PRODUCED AND BOTTLED BY
RICHARD L. GRAESER WINERY  CALISTOGA, CA.
ALCOHOL 12.9% BY VOLUME   CONTAINS SULFITES

PRODUCED AND BOTTLED BY CAFARO CELLARS, NAPA CA
CAFARO
1986
NAPA VALLEY
CABERNET SAUVIGNON
TABLE WINE · CONTAINS SULFITES

Winter Creek
WINERY
1986
NAPA VALLEY
CHARDONNAY
TAKAHASHI VINEYARD
PRODUCED & BOTTLED BY WINTER CREEK WINERY
NAPA, CALIFORNIA · BONDED WINERY 5109
ALCOHOL 13.2% BY VOLUME · CONTAINS SULFITES

FOREST HILL

BY JOANNA VINEYARD · 1987
CA — BW
JOANNA
VINEYARD
TABLE WINE
1988
NAPA VALLEY
CHARDONNAY
PRODUCED & BOTTLED
NAPA, CALIFORNIA
CONTAIN SULFITES
ALCOHOL 13% BY VOLUME

FORESTHILL
PRODUCED AND BOTTLED BY FOREST HILL VINEYARD ST HELENA CALIFORNIA 13.0° ALCOHOL BY VOLUME 750 ML
NAPA VALLEY CHARDONNAY NAPA VALLEY

Château
Napa-Beaucanon
Napa Valley
CHARDONNAY
CELLARED AND BOTTLED BY CHÂTEAU NAPA-BEAUCANON
St-HELENA · CALIFORNIA · ALCOHOL 12.8% BY VOL. · NET CONT. 750 ML

Mario Perelli-Minetti
100%
1987
Napa Valley
CHARDONNAY
Produced by M.P.M. Vineyards, Rutherford, CA, B.W. #4591
Bottled by M.P.M. Vineyards, Rutherford, CA, B.W. #5437
Alcohol 13% by volume

BERGFELD
1885
WINE CELLARS
1987
NAPA VALLEY
CHARDONNAY
ALCOHOL 13.3% BY VOLUME
PRODUCED AND BOTTLED BY BERGFELD WINE CELLARS
ST. HELENA, CALIFORNIA, CONTAINS SULFITES

LAMBORN FAMILY
VINEYARDS
NAPA VALLEY
HOWELL MOUNTAIN
ZINFANDEL
1987
GROWN, PRODUCED & BOTTLED BY LAMBORN FAMILY VINEYARDS, ANGWIN, CA
BW5389  ALCOHOL 13.6% BY VOLUME  CONTAINS SULFITES

Soda Canyon
VINEYARDS
9th Leaf
1987
Napa Valley
CHARDONNAY
PRODUCED AND BOTTLED BY SODA CANYON WINERY
ST. HELENA, CA · CONTAINS SULFITES · ALC. 13.1% BY VOL.

QUAIL RIDGE
1988
Napa Valley
Chardonnay
CELLARED AND BOTTLED BY
QUAIL RIDGE CELLARS & VINEYARDS
NAPA, CALIFORNIA   ALCOHOL 13.1% BY VOLUME

HAVENS
1987
MERLOT
NAPA VALLEY
MADE AND BOTTLED BY HAVENS WINE CELLARS
RUTHERFORD, CA ALC. 13.2% VOL. CONTAINS SULFITES

diamond creek
Red Rock Terrace
Napa 1986 Valley
Cabernet Sauvignon
grown, produced and bottled on diamond mountain by
DIAMOND CREEK VINEYARDS   CALISTOGA, CA.
ALCOHOL 12½% BY VOLUME   CONTAINS SULFITES

SPOTTSWOODE
1985
CABERNET SAUVIGNON
Napa Valley
GROWN, PRODUCED & BOTTLED BY SPOTTSWOODE VINEYARD & WINERY
OAKVILLE, CALIFORNIA, USA · CONTAINS SULFITES · ALCOHOL 13.2% BY VOLUME

1987

VINTAGE 1984          BOTTLED APRIL 1988
Bottle             of a total of 50,652 Bottles
Magnum             of a total of 1,200 Magnums
Heitz Cellar
NAPA VALLEY
CABERNET SAUVIGNON
ALCOHOL 13½% BY VOLUME
Martha's
Vineyard   PRODUCED AND BOTTLED IN OUR CELLAR BY
HEITZ WINE CELLARS
ST. HELENA, CA, U.S.A. CONTAINS SULFITES

CARNEROS
CREEK
NAPA VALLEY
Los Carneros
CHARDONNAY
PRODUCED & BOTTLED BY CARNEROS CREEK WINERY
NAPA, CALIFORNIA ALCOHOL 13.5% BY VOLUME. CONTAINS SULFITES

Steltzner
1985
ESTATE BOTTLED
NAPA VALLEY
STAGS LEAP DISTRICT
CABERNET SAUVIGNON
GROWN, PRODUCED & BOTTLED BY STELTZNER VINEYARDS,
NAPA, CALIFORNIA USA. CONTAINS SULFITES. TABLE WINE.

ESTATE BOTTLED
CHARLES SHAW
CHARDONNAY
NAPA VALLEY
GROWN, PRODUCED & BOTTLED BY CHARLES F. SHAW VINEYARD & WINERY
B.W. 4930 · ST. HELENA, CA, U.S.A. · ALC. 13.0% BY VOL. · CONTAINS SULFITES
A ROBRAND CALIFORNIA SELECTION

Aetna Springs
NAPA VALLEY
Wine Ranch
RED TABLE WINE
PRODUCED & BOTTLED BY AETNA SPRINGS WINE RANCH
POPE VALLEY, CA - ALCOHOL 12.5% BY VOLUME
CONTAINS SULFITES

S. Anderson
NAPA VALLEY
Brut
NAPA VALLEY SPARKLING WINE • PRODUCED AND BOTTLED BY S. ANDERSON VINEYARD
YOUNTVILLE, CALIFORNIA U.S.A. · B.W. 4911 ALC. 12.5% BY VOL. · NET CONTENTS 750 ML.

1985  NAPA VALLEY  MERLOT
JAEGER
INGLEWOOD VINEYARD
PRODUCED AND BOTTLED BY JAEGER CELLAR
RUTHERFORD, NAPA VALLEY, CA USA.
ALCOHOL 13% BY VOLUME

PAHLMEYER
ESTATE BOTTLED
1987
CALDWELL VINEYARD
NAPA VALLEY
A BLEND OF
CABERNET SAUVIGNON, CABERNET FRANC,
MERLOT, PETIT VERDOT & MALBEC
PRODUCED & BOTTLED BY PAHLMEYER,
ST. HELENA, CALIFORNIA

BACKUS VINEYARD
Napa Valley
Cabernet Sauvignon
1986
Joseph Phelps Vineyards
Alcohol 13.5% by volume.
Produced and bottled by Joseph Phelps Vineyards, St. Helena, Ca.

1987
DAVID ARTHUR
Vineyards
Estate Bottled
Napa Valley
CHARDONNAY
GROWN, PRODUCED & BOTTLED BY DAVID ARTHUR VINEYARDS
ST. HELENA, CA   ALC. 13.5% BY VOL.   CONTAINS SULFITES.

STERLING VINEYARDS.
ESTATE BOTTLED
1988
Sauvignon Blanc
NAPA VALLEY
GROWN, PRODUCED AND BOTTLED BY
STERLING VINEYARDS
CALISTOGA, NAPA VALLEY, CA
ALC. 12.5% BY VOL. · BW CA 4533

GARNET
1988
Carneros Pinot Noir
SAINTSBURY
PRODUCED AND BOTTLED BY SAINTSBURY, NAPA, CALIFORNIA
ALCOHOL 12.9% BY VOLUME   CONTAINS SULFITES

DUCKHORN VINEYARDS
1987
NAPA VALLEY
MERLOT
Produced and bottled by Duckhorn Vineyards
3027 Silverado Trail, St. Helena, CA 94574 BWCA 4857.
ALCOHOL 12.8% BY VOLUME. CONTAINS SULFITES

SILVER OAK®
1983
ALEXANDER VALLEY
Cabernet Sauvignon
Cellared and bottled by SILVER OAK CELLARS
Oakville, Napa County, California
Alcohol 13.6% by Volume

Beaulieu
Vineyard
BV
ESTATE BOTTLED
RUTHERFORD
NAPA VALLEY
CABERNET SAUVIGNON
PRODUCED AND BOTTLED BY BEAULIEU VINEYARD
AT RUTHERFORD, NAPA COUNTY, CALIFORNIA
ALCOHOL 12.5% BY VOLUME

62

*Preceding pages: An aerial view looks north toward Mt. St. Helena. Buildings in the lower left belong to Frog's Leap Winery; Charles Shaw Vineyards and Winery is in the center. State Highway 29 is at left and the Silverado Trail is at far right.*

*Daryl Sattui has revived his great grandfather's pre-Prohibition San Francisco winery (above top) on the south side of St. Helena. V. Sattui Winery specializes in direct sales, and offers picnic facilities to visitors who buy wine and deli goods in their retail outlet. Greystone's distinctive tower (above) graces an imposing stone building, built in 1889 and owned by the Christian Brothers since 1950. In the 1980's Greystone was reinforced to meet earthquake codes and now serves as a visitor center. A winter rainbow (left) arches over an old vineyard on Highway 29.*

*Following pages: Mustard runs riot in a vineyard near Joseph Phelps's winery in Spring Valley, a sub-valley just yards from the Silverado Trail. Later it will be plowed under to prevent the plants from taking moisture from the vines.*

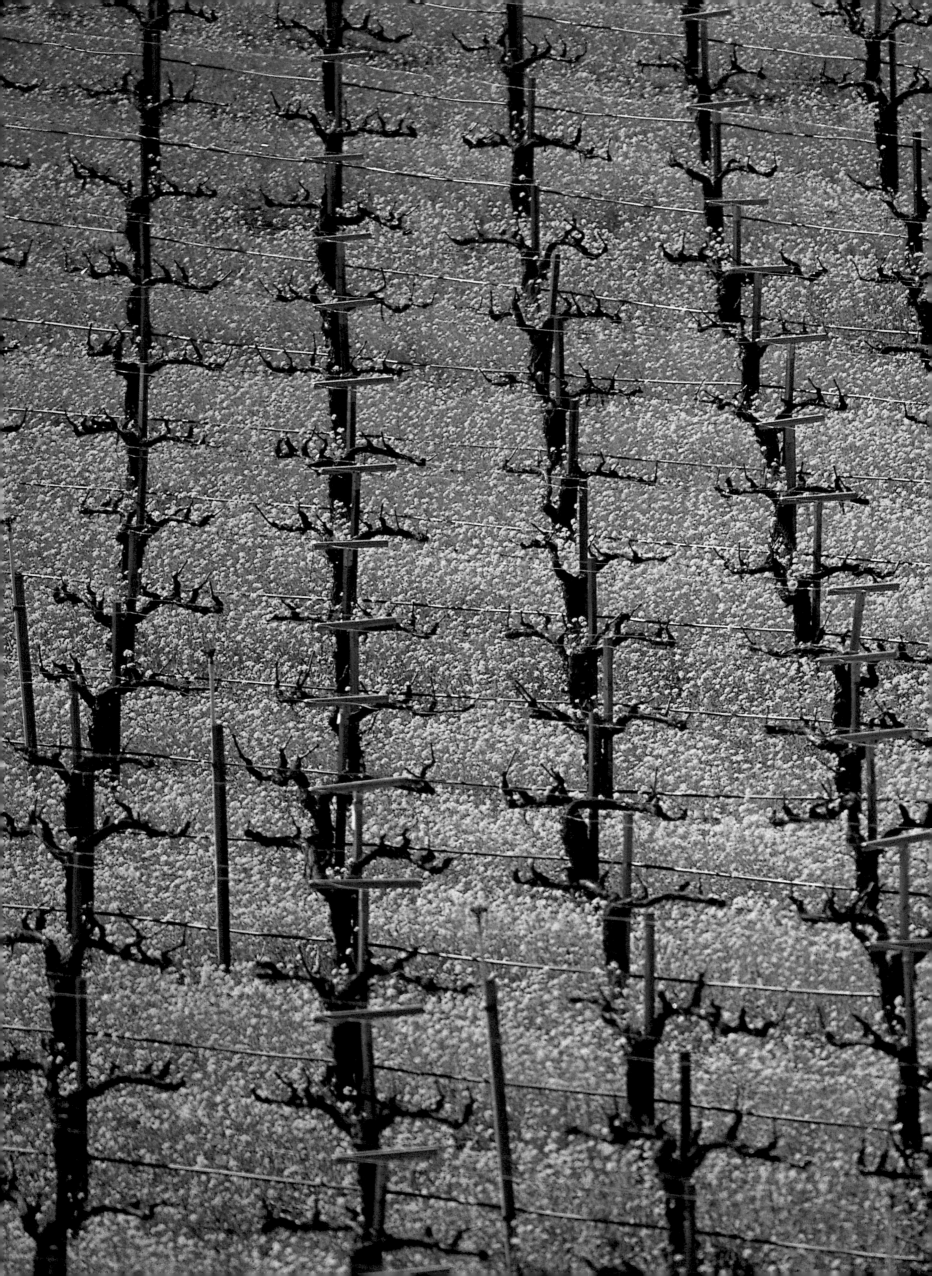

WINTER

SPRING

SUMMER

AUTUMN

# The Seasons of the Vine

NAPA VALLEY enjoys a moderate Mediterranean climate, marked at one extreme by stormy winter rains blowing in from the Pacific, and at the other by dusty-dry summer heat tempered each night by an infusion of cool marine air. Stands of olives, citrus and palm trees stamp the countryside with an Italian aura. Grapevines thrive in the relatively easy flow of the seasons and, with a consistency that Europeans envy, yield small crops of very high quality fruit. The photographs of 30-year-old zinfandel vines *(opposite)* were taken from exactly the same position at four different times of the year. The view is to the west toward the Mayacamas mountains.

WINTER *(January)*: Dormant vines, recently pruned, stand straight as sentinels and easily withstand nighttime temperatures that dip into the twenties. Daytime temperatures can reach the sixties, and the winter sun is warm enough to germinate the weed seeds in the vineyard. The rains nourish the weeds and the Valley floor is covered by several shades of green even in the middle of winter. Chief winter chore is pruning of all the vines—a vigorous trimming that removes 80%–90% of the previous year's growth.

SPRING *(March)*: Mustard ranks as everyone's favorite weed, and the Valley can be awash with Van Gogh-like yellow masses in winter and spring. As "bud break" approaches, the weeds are tilled into the soil and for a brief time the fields show bare earth, the sign of the plow. Sap begins to flow in late March or early April, and light green growth appears on the "canes" or "spurs" left on the vine after pruning. Grape growers go on nighttime vigilance for "frost season," as the next eight weeks are called. Even a light frost can decimate the year's crop. Since the vines can grow an inch a day, the floor of the Valley quickly takes on a green aspect again while the grassy hillsides turn tawny as summer approaches.

SUMMER *(July)*: When a full canopy of leaves covers the fruit, letting only filtered sunlight strike the grape clusters, the vine stops growing vegetatively and turns its energy into ripening the fruit. Soil is carefully groomed, weed free, and because of the lack of rainfall, is bone dry. In permeable soils, vines can grow deeply enough to find their own water, and for over a hundred years Napa Valley vineyards were "dry farmed." However, after two years of drought in the 1970s and near droughts in recent years, growers now install drip irrigation on most new vineyards.

AUTUMN *(October)*: "Precocious" grape varieties, such as pinot noir and gewürztraminer, are picked as early as August. Late ripening grapes, cabernet sauvignon and zinfandel, might hang on the vine until October or, in rare years, November. Colorful as the harvest might be for the visitor, winemakers and growers face enormous logistical challenges in timing the picking and managing the fermenters. In the last weeks of the harvest, rain looms as a threat to the vintage. If water penetrates to the inside of the cluster, mold starts growing and ruins the grapes for winemaking. Once the grapes are safely harvested, winter rains are welcome.

*Dormant vines near Calistoga take this February hoar-frost in stride. However, after the vines start to grow, a biting frost can seriously damage the budding grape crop.*

71

Sterling Vineyards' hilltop winery echoes the design of Greek
monasteries that rise above the Aegean Sea on island promontories.
The climate in Napa Valley is Mediterranean, warm and dry in
summer, cool and rainy in winter. The vines flourish here much as
they did ages ago when domesticated in the Middle East. Visitors
(above) to Sterling Vineyards walk on a self-guided tour through
galleries above the cellars.

Preceding pages: Splashes of color in a vineyard reveal a planting of
"mixed blacks," three or four different red grape varieties that are
picked simultaneously, effectively blending a wine in the field.

In the 19th century many wine storage caves were dug by hand. In recent years renewed demand for caves in the wine country has kept two mining machines booked for months in advance. Machine operator Don Smith (above) emerges after a day's work cutting a cave at Dunn Vineyards on Howell Mountain. At Pine Ridge Winery (left), 869 linear feet of caves keep barrels at optimum conditions of temperature and humidity without costly air conditioning. Winemaker Stacy Clark labels a barrel in a newly completed section.

Napa pioneer André Tchelistcheff makes a point in the vineyards
of Niebaum-Coppola and tastes a wine at a nearby winery.
In 1937, Georges de Latour, owner of Beaulieu Vineyards,
brought Tchelistcheff from France to make the Beaulieu wines. He
was one of the first to discover the "Rutherford Bench," a band of
prime land for cabernet sauvignon, on which he grew grapes for
many vintages named in honor of de Latour. Since retiring from
Beaulieu in 1970, he has consulted for several wineries in
California, Oregon and Washington.

Following pages: Once used as grazing land for sheep, the
undulating hills of the Los Carneros region are cooled by the
breezes off nearby San Pablo Bay, just north of San Francisco.
Cool micro-climates suit delicate grape varieties like pinot noir and
chardonnay.

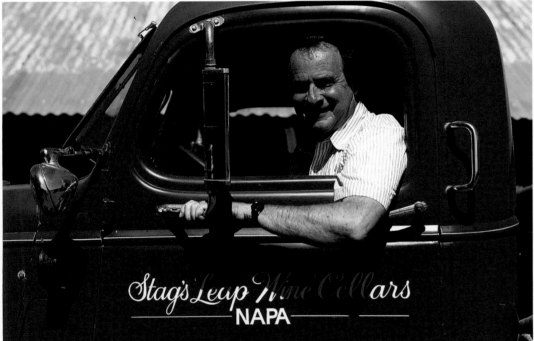

Peter Mondavi, Sr. (top), President and CEO of The Charles Krug Winery, pauses in front of the original carriage house on the Krug property. It is now used for barrel aging and special events. In the cab of an old fire truck still used to protect himself and his neighbors, Warren Winiarski (center) of Stag's Leap Wine Cellars makes it clear that a winery owner should be ready for anything. Randall Dunn (bottom), of Dunn Vineyards, stands beside a parcel of his land just cleared for planting more Howell Mountain cabernet sauvignon.

Striking both in form and color, Clos Pegase (right) makes a strong statement in the vineyards just south of Calistoga. Architect Michael Graves won a design competition sponsored by the San Francisco Museum of Modern Art by designing a building that functions as both winery equipped to make premium wine and as gallery for owner Jan Shrem's art collection.

*"Johanna II," the super-sized portrait of a blond woman (above) is one piece in The Hess Collection, a winery and art gallery on Mt. Veeder. Swiss businessman Donald Hess devoted two years to renovating the 19th-century winery building previously used by The Christian Brothers. Visitors can stroll through the art galleries as part of their winery tour. Vineyards provide a dramatic background (left) for a private luncheon under the palms at Spottswoode Winery.*

At Meadowood Resort Hotel (above), just outside St. Helena,
guests play croquet on lawns built to international specifications.
Steve Bell, a local vineyard manager, stomps grapes (left) against a
time clock as part of the St. Helena Hometown Harvest Festival.

Preceding pages: The 98-year-old Ritchie Block building is reflected in a
window of the weekly newspaper, the 116-year-old St. Helena Star.

Following pages: Wine and food enthusiasts gather at Merryvale
Vineyards for candlelight lunches and dinners in an Old World
atmosphere that features rows of old casks.

The spas and mud baths of Calistoga (above) have been popular
since the middle of the 19th century. In 1862, Sam Brannan, a
colorful entrepreneur, developed an elaborate Victorian Resort in the
Hot Springs Township of Calistoga. Concerts at Robert Mondavi
Winery range from Chopin, played by Richard Secrist, for a small
group (top) in the "Vineyard Room" to jazz performed on the lawn
for 1,500 guests (left).

"Making good wine is a skill, making fine wine is an art," says Robert Mondavi, whose enthusiastic promotions of both the Napa Valley and premium wines lead many people to consider him America's ambassador to the international wine world. His mission-style winery (above), built in Oakville in 1966, was the first winery constructed after Prohibition. It pays tribute to the Spanish fathers who brought grapes and wine into California in the late 18th century. The winery accommodates more than 160,000 visitors annually, and hosts scores of cultural events. Mondavi's wife, Margrit Biever, stands with him in their home (left), a mirror image of the winery's architecture. Barrel room foreman Manny Martinez (far left) inspects a 500-gallon German oval cask used for aging white wine. The extensive use of European cooperage was one of Mondavi's earliest contributions to the wine industry.

*Following pages: A winter scene along the Silverado Trail.*

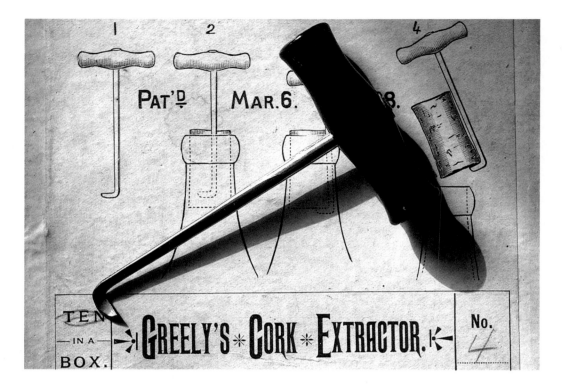

*A bag of corks (above) ready for the bottling line. A discovery about 200 years ago showed that the resilience of cork made a nearly perfect seal, allowing wine to age in bottles. Extracting the cork became a challenge, and hundreds of devices, like the cork extractor (above top) in the museum at St. Supery Vineyards and Winery, have been designed to facilitate the task. An old water tower near Oakville (left) is shrouded in early morning fog.*

*Following pages: Bottles of old Pinot Noir and Cabernet Sauvignon rest in a special corner of Beringer Vineyards' caves. The bottles date back to the years just after Prohibition, which lasted from 1919 to 1933.*

# Cellaring Wine

OF ALL THE FEATURES that mark wine as a unique beverage, aging, or its gradual changing over time, is perhaps the most fascinating. Unfortunately, the notion of aging is misunderstood and even intimidates many people. Part of the problem lies in the commonplace notion that each wine has a "peak" of enjoyment at some precise point in time. It's almost a threat: If you miss the "peak" you have ruined the wine.

In fact, most of the wine made in the world actually asks for no aging at all. This includes ninety per cent of white wine and as much as fifty per cent of red wine. Those wines have been called "weekday wine"; they need only be fresh and clean tasting.

Napa Valley and a number of other small winegrowing regions in the world have the good fortune to enjoy soils and climates that make "Sunday wine"—wines that show more character and flavor than ordinary wines. Because such climates often provide good vintages, the wines that result usually profit from some aging.

The basic questions about aging are: "How long? For which wines?" Answers are best given on a regional basis, though the guidelines for Napa Valley will not be wildly different from those in other California regions. A good wine merchant will be able to explain the aging periods for Bordeaux, Burgundy, Chianti, etc.

Cabernet Sauvignon and Chardonnay are often called king and queen of today's Napa Valley, partly because these varieties have the best aging potential.

The idea of "peak" is particularly misleading to winedrinkers; "plateau" makes more sense. For Chardonnay, the plateau can last three to five years, as an average. For Cabernet Sauvignon, eight to ten years. Some Chardonnays develop a little more quickly; a few Cabernets last much longer. At age 45, an Inglenook Cask Cabernet offered unbelieveably fine flavors and

showed no signs of deterioration!

Deciding when to open a bottle still remains a personal judgment. For being patient with Chardonnays, the rewards are fuller, more complex flavors and less of the grapey-fruitiness of youth. With Cabernets, and other red wines, subtle, perfumey fragrances replace grape and oak aromas and the "mouth feel" gradually changes from puckery and aggressive to a softer, suppler way of delivering the wine's flavors.

A cellar needn't be large or expensive. The changes we call aging happen best under stable conditions—cooler temperatures, low light, minimal movement. Interior closets make decent cellars in most regions. Temperature affects aging most significantly. Wine stored at 70° F will age almost twice as fast as wine stored at 55° F, but it will *not* be ruined.

A cellar is best started as a collection, a stable, of one's favorite Sunday wines, several bottles each of five or six wines. Red wines that require less time than Cabernet, Pinot Noir and Merlot, will show quicker results. Some Sauvignon Blancs show as much aging potential as Chardonnay.

A person can be aggressive about building a cellar by reading wine newsletters and new release columns in magazines. Or, with a marketplace full of good wines, simply let new wines work their way into the stable after encounters in restaurants or at friends' homes. A cellar, large or small, calculated or casual, has only the job of bringing an element of discovery and some extra pleasures to the Sunday table—even if it happens to be Wednesday night.

*At Schramsberg Vineyards (right) more than two million bottles of sparkling wine age in caves dug by hand in the 1880's. Sparkling wine, or champagne as many people call it, receives its aging at the winery. Once the bottle reaches the retail shelf, it is fully ready to enjoy.*

Hands of a cellarworker (above) tell the story: he's been emptying
red wine from a press. A classic Victorian house (left) now serves as
reception center and offices for St. Clement Vineyards. Similar
houses, large and small, dot the Napa Valley, and reflect the
architecture brought to northern California after the gold rush of the
mid-1800's.

Following pages:Vines and grape stakes line up as sunset silhouettes
on the crest of a hill in Los Carneros.

Hugo Robledo Morales, cooper at Tonnellerie Francaise-French Cooperage of America in Calistoga (above), drives a hoop down on unbent staves. The staves are positioned over a fire which heats the oak, enabling the cooper to bend the stave with a winch. By means of an ingenious "router on a roller skate," used barrels can be renewed. At Barrel Builders in St. Helena (right), co-owner Henry Work guides the router and shaves off one-eighth inch of wine-impregnated wood to expose a fresh oak surface. Oak barrels play a major role in making Cabernet Sauvignon, Chardonnay, Sauvignon Blanc and Pinot Noir, the chief wines of Napa Valley. For the winemaker, oak becomes part of his winemaking strategy. Theories about the "right" oak and its use vary widely. French oak or American oak? New barrels or older barrels? Six months of aging, 12 months, or 24 months? Finally, theory and practicality compromise—French barrels cost as much as $500 each; American barrels half as much—and each wine gets its "seasoning" of oak.

Fourth-generation winemaker Hanns Kornell (above) sits on a porch outside the offices at his winery on Larkmead Lane. Kornell was raised in the Rhine Valley of Germany, where his family produced both still and sparkling wines. He served as apprentice to Champagne producers in France and to vintners in Italy before he emigrated to the United States in 1940. Here he served as Champagne master for other producers until he founded Hanns Kornell Champagne Cellars in 1952.

Stuart Smith and his brother Charles (left) lean against a row of barrels as they talk about the wine they've been tasting. They evaluate wines from the barrels, using the "wine thief" that Charles holds in his left hand. Smith-Madrone Vineyards and Winery, a family run business, has been making wine since 1977.

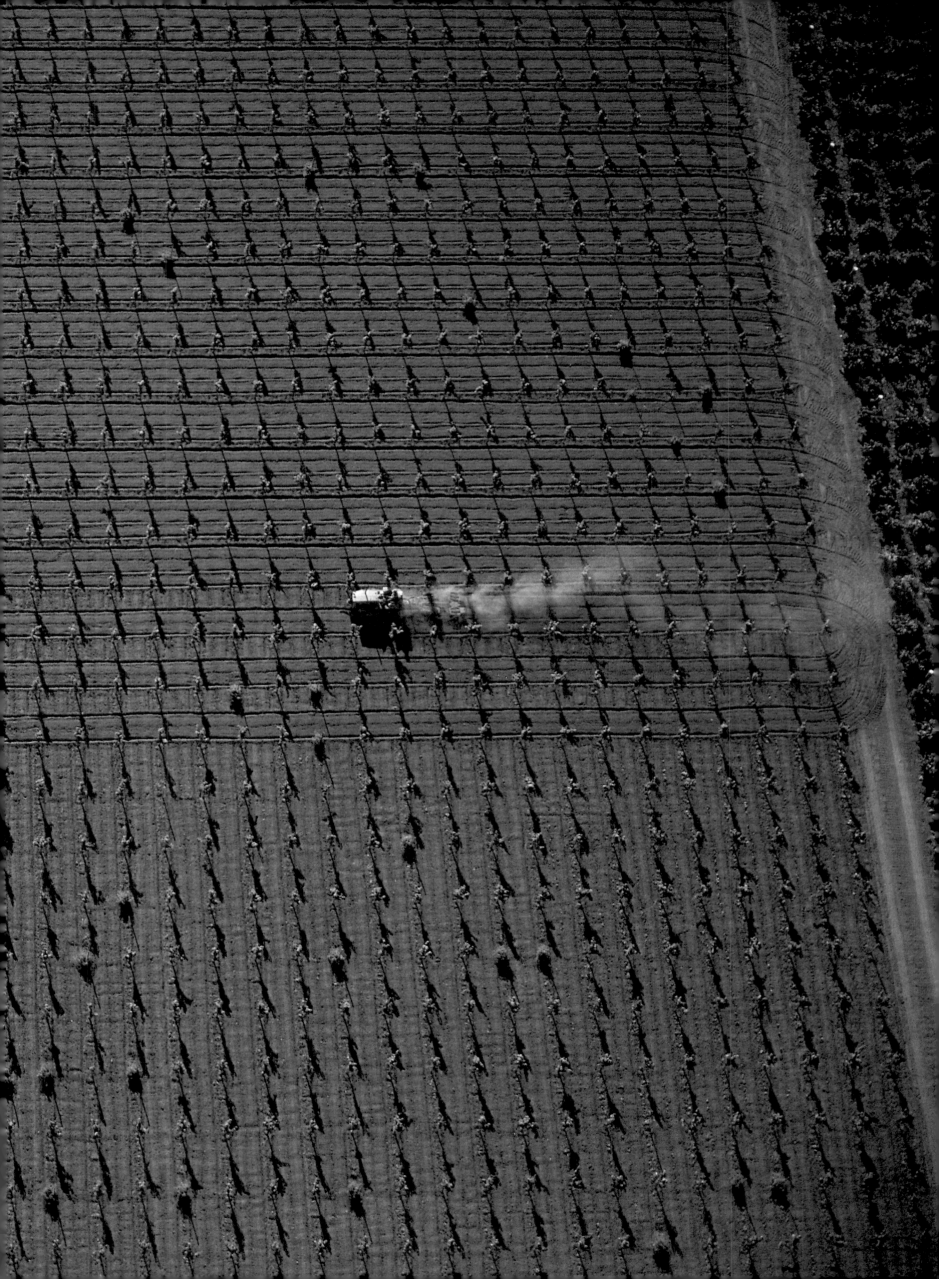

Unfolding like a delicate green fan (above), the buds on a cane of pinot noir begin the vine's five-to-six-month growing season. If a cane is cut from a vine and kept in cold storage to prevent its sprouting, individual buds can be cut from it as "chips" for propagating new vines. In August the chip is inserted into a V-shaped notch (above top) in the trunk of previously planted rootstock. The next spring, after "bud break," the chip bud will grow up from the rootstock, producing a new vine. Pruning the dormant grape vines (right) keeps vineyard crews busy most of the winter. Up to ninety per cent of the previous year's growth is removed. Knowing the number of buds left on the vine (each bud usually produces two clusters) and the number of vines per acre, growers can determine the tonnage for the upcoming vintage.

Preceding pages: A tractor cross-tills a vineyard near Yountville early in the season, before the vines are grown.

From bud break in late March until May, the threat of frost hangs over the vineyard. Juan Zago lights burners near Rutherford (left), and establishes one line of defense. Warming the air just a few degrees can protect the tender shoots. On windless nights cold air settles on the vines. Wind machines, huge engines with propellers (above), stir up the air mass over the vineyard; the warmer upper air brings some relief. In recent years, vineyards have been outfitted with overhead sprinklers which sprinkle the entire vineyard with water to protect the vines from frost damage.


Preceding pages: An unusual September rain storm sweeps through the hills east of Oakville, heading toward Atlas Peak.

*Chimney Rock Winery (above), constructed in the Cape Dutch
style, rests below hillside vineyards along the Silverado Trail, north
of Napa. Far Niente Winery (top) undertook an extensive
renovation of a 19th-century stone winery to begin its winemaking
in 1979. Recently, owner Gil Nickel cut 1,000 linear feet of caves
out of the hill below the winery. In Spring Valley, rows of cabernet
sauvignon (foreground) and sauvignon blanc owned by Joseph Phelps
Vineyards run in directions that suit the contours of the hills.
Twenty years ago, cattle grazed the same land.*

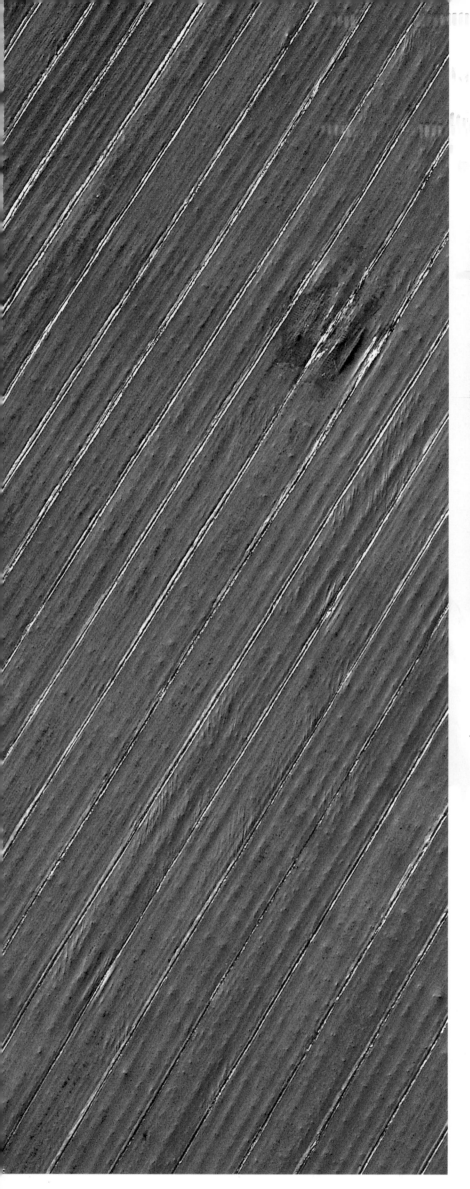

In the final step of preparing the soil for a new vineyard (left), a tractor spreads plastic sheeting that will hold a fumigant in the earth for a few weeks. Without the treatment, young vines would be attacked quickly by nematodes, parasitic worms. A tractor driver, Guadalupe Maldonado (above), samples some of the harvest in one of Schramsberg's vineyards.

Peering through a refractometer, Tom Burgess (top) measures the sugar content of grapes in his ripening vineyard. Donn Chappellet (above) stands near stainless steel fermenters in his winery on Pritchard Hill. Both men farm the eastern slopes of the Napa Valley: Chappellet since 1967, Burgess since 1972. At Sutter Home Winery, on Zinfandel Lane (left), tanks containing 25,000 gallons of wine loom toward the sky, as Terry Baughman looks down from a high catwalk.

*Looking like a simple country store, the Oakville Grocery (right) draws gourmets the way flowers attract bees. A small section of the cheeses (above) hints at the breadth of selection that extends to pâté, sausages, fruits and vegetables, wine and delectable desserts for wine country picnics. Three entrepreneurs of taste—Ann Grace, Susan Simpson, and Ruth Rydman (top) created the Napa Valley Mustard Company in 1982, and now market three mustards and a catsup under their label.*

In St. Helena, the distinctive Rhine House at Beringer Vineyards (left) echoes the architecture of the founder's home near Mainz, Germany. Inside the Rhine House are offices, several tasting rooms and a retail shop for the 200,000 visitors who come to the winery each year.

The ivy on the walls of Beaulieu Vineyard casts an autumnal and almost collegiate look to the scene, as do the leaves dropping from the ash trees. Inside is one of the few wineries that survived during Prohibition by making sacramental wines.

Shadows of fermenters frame the door of a "chai" (left), at Duckhorn Vineyards. An architectural concept borrowed from Bordeaux, France, the chai is a set of simple low buildings designed specifically for aging wine in barrels.

Following pages: Working in his old stone winery, Angelo Regusci crafts unique wines for himself and his family by creatively blending wines made from different grape varieties.

Napa Valley features a bounty of architectural traditions.
Inglenook's winery building (top) in Rutherford was constructed in
1882 and now serves as a visitor center and historical cellar for
bottles dating back to the same year. The giant stone winery
building on the Regusci Ranch (above) was built in 1878. Mustard
blossoms seem to point through vine rows to a water tower (right) on
the Rossi property on Highway 29 near St. Helena.

Following pages: Lush fields of grain roll across hills in Los
Carneros. Grain and hay fields are giving way to vineyards, as
demand keeps increasing for Napa Valley wines.

The Napa Valley Wine Auction (above), held each June at Meadowood Resort Hotel, is sponsored by the Napa Valley Vintners Association, an organization representing the majority of valley wineries. The auction has become world-famous, and raises funds for three Napa Valley health care facilities. Bidding proceeds from midday to early evening in a tent (far left) large enough to seat 1,500 people. The tent also shelters a gala dinner on the eve of the auction. Smaller auctions in the valley raise funds for many local causes. Three bottles of Conn Creek Cabernet Sauvignon (left) attract written bids in a silent auction.

137

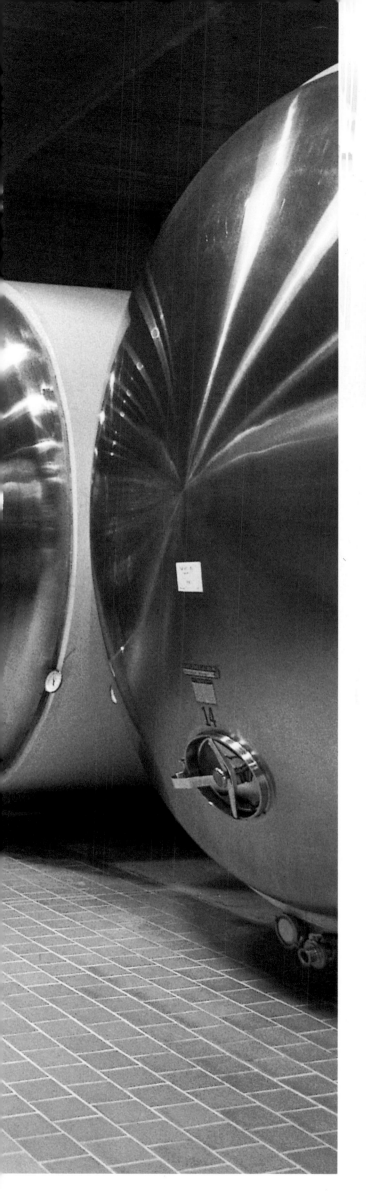

*Visitors to the Robert Mondavi Winery (above) end their tour with an intimate tasting as a guide provides pointers on appreciating the aromas, bouquets and flavors. At Domaine Chandon (left) a tour group pauses in the curvilinear fermentation room where stainless steel fermenters, with polished ends and insulated sides, lie horizontally. Approximately two million people visit Napa County each year, most to enjoy the scenic vineyards, wineries and restaurants.*

*Jack Davies (above) bought the original Jacob Schram property in
1965 and established Schramsberg Vineyards. Davies and his wife
Jamie restored both the winery and Schram's home, originally built in
1875. Production has grown gradually to include five sparkling
wines, for a total of 45,000 cases per year. In a half-full glass of
Chardonnay (left), the image of a water tower and barn turns upside
down and takes on the gold-green hue of the wine.*

*Following pages: Along the Silverado Trail mustard weeds in bloom
make the vineyards glow yellow in early spring.*

Dew drops stand out on cabernet sauvignon grapes (above) in late summer. The berries are magnified ten times normal size. A hand holds a cluster in bloom (right), revealing the minute size of a grape flower. Harvesting at the Grace Family Vineyard is an affair for family and friends: Tia O'Rear (far right) focuses on cutting the stem of a cabernet sauvignon cluster. Annual production is 350 cases of Cabernet Sauvignon from two acres of vineyards near the Grace's home.

*The varied shapes of California live oak trees (above) create some of Napa Valley's distinctive visual textures. Their asymmetry emerges when the sun sets on the Silverado Trail. Near Taplin Road, a single live oak (left) crowns a hillside covered with California poppies* (Eschscholzia californica) *and wild hyacinths* (Brodiaea capitata).

From his jeep, Peter Newton (above) scans growth in the vineyards on his hillside ranch. High above St. Helena, formal gardens (left) promenade on top of Newton's buried barrel aging room. Conditions in the room are like those in a cave. In 1964, Newton entered the wine business when he founded Sterling Vineyards. After he and his partners sold Sterling Vineyards to The Coca-Cola Company in 1977, Newton purchased a 560-acre property out of which he has carved 100 steeply sloping acres of vines for the wines of Newton Vineyards.

*Wine industry patriarch Louis P. Martini (above) surveys one of his easternmost vineyards, located in Pope Valley. The Martini family arrived in Napa Valley in 1933, and has operated the winery for three generations. Martini's father, Louis M. Martini, developed one of the first vineyards in Los Carneros in 1948, and also planted two vineyards in Sonoma County. Primarily intended for frost protection, overhead sprinklers (left) may also be used for cooling vineyards on the hottest of days, and for irrigation when the water supply is adequate.*

*Following pages: Morning sun highlights drip irrigation lines hanging below a three-wire trellis system on the Silverado Trail, near the Yountville Crossroad. Later in the growing season, the elongated canes are tied onto the two upper wires, opening the clusters at the center of the vine to better air circulation and additional sunlight.*

*Looking north in the Oakville area clearly shows how vineyards get planted in "blocks." Reservoirs, like the one at top center, normally fill with winter rains and with water pumped from wells and from the Napa River. The water will be used as frost protection and for irrigation during the dry growing season.*

*In 1967, Chuck Carpy (top) was one of the founding partners of Freemark Abbey Winery and, a few years later, of Rutherford Hill Winery. Carpy's grandfather came to the Napa Valley from Bordeaux, France in 1864. Eleanor McCrea (above) and her late husband Fred founded Stony Hill Vineyard in 1953 and initiated the era of the small premium winery. Production started at 150 cases and has grown to 4,000 cases per year. Today wine buyers face a four-year wait just to get on the mailing list for Stony Hill's new releases.*

Milk cartons (above) protect tender new growth from harsh elements
and pests such as rabbits, while vines climb up stakes during the
first year of growth. As Napa Valley acreage devoted to wine has
increased over the last 25 years, the number of grape varieties has
diminished. Now three white varieties, chardonnay, sauvignon
blanc and chenin blanc, and four red varieties, cabernet sauvignon,
pinot noir, merlot and zinfandel, account for 88% of the Valley's
total grape bearing area of approximately 28,000 acres. On the
west side of St. Helena (right), a vineyard climbs a hill behind a
farm building topped by an old schoolhouse bell. The family of
Bud Meyer owns the vineyard, called Madrone Ranch, a hillside
acreage of cabernet sauvignon planted by vineyardist David Abreu.

*Napa Valley ranks as the busiest hot air ballooning corridor in North America. Weather conditions in the Valley dictate early morning flights. On a busy morning as many as 25 balloons dot the sky.*

*Sporting color for a festival in Los Carneros, Rene di Rosa (below) performs a familiar role: organizing events in order to preserve agricultural land. He planted Winery Lake Vineyard in 1962, and at one time sold his grapes to 17 wineries.*

*Joe Heitz (above) examines the hue and clarity of one of his wines with the practiced eye of an expert. Heitz celebrated the 25th anniversary of Heitz Wine Cellars in 1986. Before starting his own winery, Heitz taught enology at Fresno State University, worked for E. & J. Gallo and was understudy to André Tchelistcheff at Beaulieu Vineyard. Heitz has been a successful promoter of single vineyard wines, those from a particular plot of land. His "Martha's Vineyard" and "Bella Oaks" Cabernet Sauvignons are Napa Valley classics.*

*Following pages: The slopes of Sterling Vineyards' Diamond Mountain Ranch above Calistoga look gentle from above, but are so steep in places that a person standing on one terrace sees at eye level the roots of vines just one row uphill.*

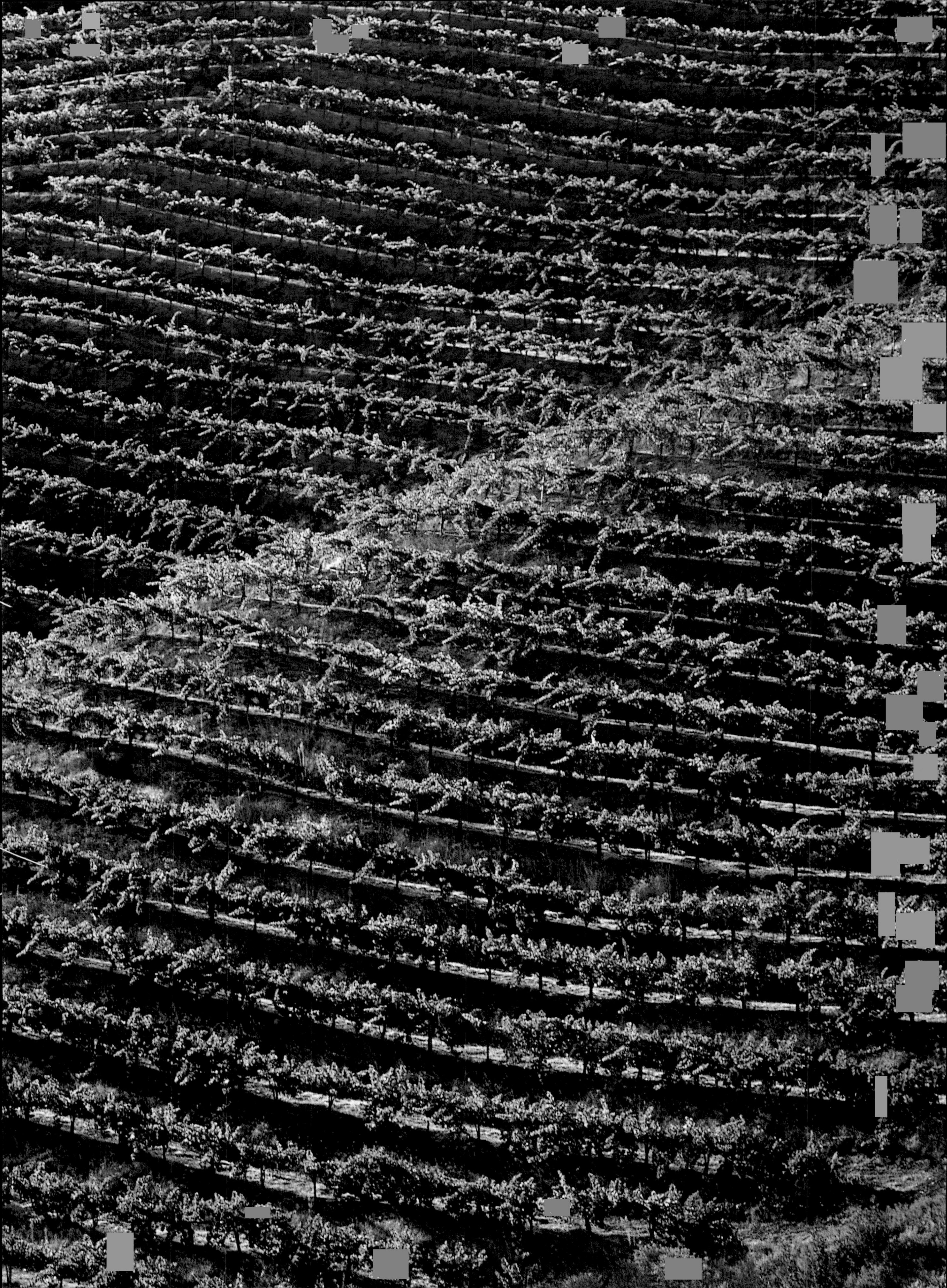

At St. Supéry Vineyards and Winery (right), the 19th-century Atkinson House has been restored as a museum that documents the life-style of a grape-growing country gentleman in the late 1800's. St. Supery is owned by the Skallis, a family active in the French wine business and food industry. They planted their first local vineyard in 1982, and opened the winery to the public in 1989. Lights come on at Domaine Carneros (top) as the sun sets. A joint venture between Champagne Taittinger from France and Kobrand, an American wine and spirits marketing company, Domaine Carneros produces only sparkling wine. The building is a duplicate of the "Chateau de la Marquetterie," an estate Taittinger owns in the Champagne district of France. At Spring Mountain Vineyards (above), Michael Robbins restored the Parrott mansion as his home, which later became the setting for the television drama, "Falcon Crest." Currently Robbins produces wine under two labels: Falcon Crest and Spring Mountain.

*A cabernet sauvignon leaf (above) is illuminated by sun penetrating morning fog. On the Smith-Madrone ranch (left), rows of johannisberg riesling vines curve toward a fog bank. Forty-three-hundred-foot Mt. St. Helena gives a ghostly presence as it stands ten miles away. The mountain forms the northern end of Napa Valley.*

*Following pages: Clusters of cabernet sauvignon hang near ripeness in the Grace Family Vineyard.*

# Index

Abreu, David, 156
Acacia, 53, *label 63*
Aetna Springs Wine Ranch, *label 60*
Alicante Bouschet, xvi, xxi
Alta Vineyard Cellar, *label 56*
Altamura, *label 55*
Amizetta Vineyards, *label 56*
Anderson, S. Vineyard, 48-49, *label 60*
Arroyo, Vincent Winery, *label 57*
Arthur, David Vineyards, *label 60*
Atkinson House, 162, 163
Atlas Peak, 116-117, 119

Bancroft, *label 61*
Barrel Builders, 108, 109
BATF, 53
Baughman, Terry, 124, 125
Beaulieu Vineyard, xvi, xvii, xx, *label 60*, 78,
    128, 129, 159
Bell, Steve, 88, 89
Bella Oaks Cabernet Sauvignon, 159
Bergfeld Wine Cellars, *label 59*
Beringer: brothers, xvii; Jacob, xvi; Vineyards, i,
    xii, xvi, xvii, xxi, xxii, *label 57*, 99, 100-101, 129
Bertolucci, Connie, 50, 51
Biever, Margrit, 95
Bouchaine, *label 57*
Bud break, 71, 114, 119
Buehler Vineyards, *label 63*
Burgess: Cellars, *label 58*; Tom, 125
Burgundy grapes, xxi

Cabernet Sauvignon, i, ivv, x, xvi, xx, xxi, 4, 5,
    53, 71, 78, 82, 99, 100-101, 108, 120-121, 137,
    144, 145, 156, 159, 165, 166-167
Cadman, Bill, 42
Cafaro, *label 59*
Cain, *label 63*
Cakebread: Cellars, 20, 25; *label 55*; Jack, 20
Calafia Cellars, *label 61*
California live oak, 146, 147
California poppies, 146, 147
California Soleil Vineyards, *label 55*
Calistoga, xiv, xv, 71, 82, 93, 108, 159
Cap, 40, 41
Cape Dutch architecture, 120
Caporale, *label 63*
Carignane, xvi, xxi
Carneros Creek, *label 60*
Carpy, Chuck, 155
Carrillo, Francisco, 8, 9
Casa Nuestra, *label 61*
Caymus Vineyards, *label 54*
Ceja, Pablo, 40, 41
Chai, 129
Champagne Taittinger, 162
Champagne, 102, 111, 162
Chanter, *label 61*
Chappellet: Donn, *label 56*, 125; Vineyard, xx,
    36-37, 46-47, 48, 125
Chardonnay, xx, xxi, xxii, 6-7, 8, 20, 21, 25, 34-
    35, 36, 41, 53, 78, 102, 108, 140, 141, 156
Chateau Chevre, *label 54*
Chateau Montelena, xx, *label 58*
Chateau Napa-Beaucanon, *label 59*
Chateau Potelle, *label 62*
Chateau Woltner, *label 63*
Chenin Blanc, 156
Chiles Valley, xiv, xv

Chimney Rock Winery, *label 52*, 120
Christian Brothers, The, 4, *label 57*, 67. 85
Clark, Stacy, 76, 77
Clos du Val, *label 58*
Clos Pegase, xii, *label 52*, 53, 82-83
Coit, Lily Hitchcock, xv, xxi
Colby Vineyards, *label 59*
Colonna, Ralph, 53
Conn Creek, *label 57*, 137
Conn Valley Vineyards, *label 62*
Cosentino, *label 63*
Costello Vineyards, *label 61*
Crichton Hall, *label 62*
Cuvaison, *label 57*

Dalla Valle Vineyards, *label 62*
Davies, Jack, Jamie, xx, 141
de Latour, Georges, xvii, 78
Deer Park Winery, *label 56*
Del Arroyo, Mark, 36, 39
DeMoor, *label 63*
di Rosa, Rene, 159
Diamond Creek, *label 60*
Diamond Mountain Ranch, xxi, 159, 160-161
Diamond Mountain Road, 30-31, 33
Domaine Carneros, xii, 162
Domaine Chandon, xii, 25, *label 63*, 138-139
Domaine Montreaux, *label 61*
Domaine Napa, *label 61*
Dominus Estate, *label 54*
Drip irrigation, 6-7, 71, 151, 152-153
Duckhorn: Dan, 29; Vineyards, 28, 29, *label 60*,
    129
Dunn: Randall, 82; Vineyards, *label 56*, 77, 82
Dusinberré *label 54*

El Molino, *label 61*
Estate Bottled, 53
Etude, *label 62*
Evensen, *label 54*

Fairmont Cellars, *label 62*
Falcon Crest, 162
Far Niente Winery, *label 55*, 120
Fermenter(s), xix, 33, 36, 38-39, 40-41, 71, 125,
    129, 138-139
Flora Springs, *label 56*
Folie à Deux, *label 57*
Forest Hill, *label 59*
Forman, *label 56*
Franciscan, *label 61*
Freemark Abbey Winery, xx, 8, 20, *label 63*, 155
Fremont Creek, *label 52*
Frisinger Cellars, *label 62*
Frog's Leap Winery, *label 55*, 64, 67
Frost: protection, 151, 155; season, 71, 119

Galleron, Gary, 48, 49
Gewurztraminer, 71
Gier, Theo. Winery, xix
Girard, *label 59*
Gondola, 14, 15, 16-17, 36
Goosecross, *label 63*
Grace Family Vineyards, *label 58*, 144, 165
Grace, Ann, 126
Graeser, *label 59*
Grapecrusher, The, 170
Graves, Michael, 82
Green & Red Vineyard, *label 54*
Greystone Cellars, xii, 67
Grgich Hills, *label 57*
Groth, *label 52*

Hagafen, *label 61*
Harvest(ing)(ed), 4, 14, 18, 36, 71, 123, 144

Havens, *label 60*
Heitz: Joe, xx, 159; Wine Cellars, xx, *label 60*, 159
Hess: Collection, The, xix, *label 57*, 85; Donald, 85
Hill, William, *label 63*
Honig, *label 63*
Hopper(s), 2-3, 4, 26-27, 29, 30-31, 33
Hot air balloons, 158, 159
Howell Mountain, xxi, 77, 82
Hunter Ashby, *label 63*
Hydrometer, 41

Inglenook, xii, xvi, xvii, xxii, *label 63*, 102, 132
Innisfree, *label 62*
Insignia, 53

Jaeger, *label 60*
Joanna Vineyard, *label 59*
Johannisberg Riesling, 164, 165
Johns, Dennis, viii, x
Johnson Turnbull, *label 58*

Kate's Vineyard, *label 59*
Keenan, Robert, *label 55*
Kornell: Hanns, 111; Hanns Champagne Cellars,
    *label 54*, 111
Krug: Charles, xvi, xvii; Charles Winery, xvi,
    xvii, xx, *label 52*, 82

La Croix, *label 62*
La Jota Vineyard Co., *label 63*
La Vieille Montagne, *label 61*
Lakespring, *label 56*
Lamborn Family Vineyards, *label 59*
Larkmead Lane, 111
Larkmead, xv, xxi
Leon, Julian, 19
Lichine, Alexis, 53
Limur, *label 62*
Livingston, *label 56*
Llords & Elwood, *label 62*
Long Vineyards, *label 55*
Los Carneros, xxi, 22-23, 25, 78, 80-81, 105,
    106-107, 132, 134-135, 137, 151, 159
Luper, J.E., *label 55*

Macauley, *label 59*
Madrone Ranch, 156, 157
Maldonado, Guadalupe, 123
Manzanita, *label 54*
Markham, *label 55*
Marston Vineyard, *label 59*
Martha's Vineyard Cabernet Sauvignon, xxi, 159
Martinez, Manny, 94, 95
Martini, Louis M. winery, 14, 40, 41, 48, 50-51,
    53, *label 61*
Martini: family, xvi, xvii, 151; Louis M., 151;
    Louis P., 151
Mayacamas, *label 61*
Mayacamas, range, mountains, xiv, xv, 71
McCrea, Eleanor, 155
Meadowood Resort Hotel, xxii, 89, 137
Mechanical harvester(ing), 22-23, 24, 25, 26-27, 29
Merlion, *label 54*
Merlot, Marilyn, *label 61*
Merlot, xx, xxi, 102, 156
Merryvale Vineyards, *label 58*, 90-91, 93
Meyer, Bud, 156
Milat Vineyards, *label 52*
Miles, Gino, 170
Mondavi family, xvi, xvii
Mondavi, Cesare, Helen, Mary, Rosa, xvii
Mondavi, Robert Winery, xii, xvii, xxii, 33, *label 55*,
    92, 93, 139
Mondavi: Peter Sr., xvii, 82; Robert, xvii, xx, 95
Mont La Salle, 2-3, 4

Mont St. John, *label 57*
Monticello Cellars, *label 58*
Morales, Hugo Robledo, 108
Moss Creek, *label 62*
Mount Veeder Winery, *label 58*
Mt. St. Helena, xiv, xv, 64, 67, 164, 165
Mt. Veeder, xxi, 85
Mumm: Cuvée Napa, *label 56*; G.H., 36; Napa
  Valley 34–35, 36
Munoz, Salvador, 12, 13
Mustard, 67, 68–69, 71, 132, 133, 141, 142–143

Napa Cellars, *label 63*
Napa Creek Winery, *label 52*
Napa Gamay, xxi
Napa Valley Mustard Company, 126
Napa Valley Port Cellars, *label 62*
Napa Valley Vintners Association, xxii, 137
Napa Valley Wine Auction, xxii, 136, 137
Napa Vintners Brand, *label 62*
Napa, city of, 4, 120
Newlan Vineyards & Winery, *label 54*
Newton: Peter, xx, 149; Vineyards, i, ii–iii, *label 52,*
  148–149
Neyers, *label 59*
Nickel, Gil, 120
Niebaum-Coppola, *label 61*, 78–79
Niebaum: Gustave, xvi, xvii; Gustave Collection,
  *label 56*
Nouveau wine, 36

O'Rear, Tia, 144, 145
Oak, American, 108
Oak, French, x, xx, 46–47, 48, 108
Oakville Grocery, 126–127
Oakville, xx, 95, 99, 119, 155
Opus One, 53, *label 57*

Pahlmeyer, *label 60*
Parrott: mansion, 162; Tiburcio, xii
Pecota, Robert, 36, *label 57*
Peju, *label 57*
Pepi, Robert, *label 63*
Perelli-Minetti, Mario, *label 59*
Perez, L. & Sons, *label 59*
Peschon, Francoise, 41
Pestoni, Bob, 44, 45
Petite Sirah, xxi
Phelps, Joseph Vineyards, *label 60, 67, 120*
Phylloxera, xvi, xx, xxi
Pina Cellars, *label 55*
Pine Ridge Winery, *label 55,* 76–77
Pinot Noir, xvi, xx, xxi, 14, 16–17, 71, 78, 99,
  100–101, 102, 108, 114, 156
Plam Vineyards, *label 58*
Pomace, 33, 44–45
Pope Valley Winery, *label 56*
Pope Valley, xiv, xv, 151
Pradel, Bernard Cellars, *label 56*
Prager, *label 52*
Presten Produce, Poultry & Wine Co., *label 56*
Private Reserve, 53
Prohibition, xv, xvi, xvii, xx, xxi, 8, 67, 95, 99, 129
Pruning, 71, 114, 115
Pumping over, 40, 41

Quail Ridge, *label 60*

R Cellars, *label 61*
Rasmussen, Kent Winery, *label 55*
Raymond, *label 57*
Red Barn Ranch, 20, 21
Regusci: Angelo, 129, 130–131; Ranch, 132
Revere, *label 58*
Rhine House, xii, 128, 129

Rhine Valley, 111
Ritchie Block building, 86–87, 89
Ritchie Creek Vineyard, *label 52*
RMS, *label 54*
Robbins, Michael, 162
Robinson, Paul, 48
Rombauer Vineyards, *label 57*
Rossi water tower, 132, 133
Round Hill, *label 58*
Rustridge, *label 58*
Rutherford Bench, 78
Rutherford Hill Winery, 8, *label 63*, 155
Rutherford Vintners, *label 61*
Rutherford, 20, 26–27, 29, 119, 132
Rydman, Ruth, 126

Saddleback Cellars, *label 58*
Saintsbury, *label 60*
San Francisco Museum of Modern Art, 82
San Pablo Bay, xiv, xv, xxi, 78
San Pietro Vara, *label 57*
Sattui: Daryl, 67; V. Winery, *label 55*, 67
Sauvignon Blanc, xxi, 102, 108, 120–121, 156
Schram, Jacob, xvii, 141
Schramsberg Vineyards, xx, *label 62*, 102, 103,
  123, 141
Schug Cellars, *label 57*
Schuster, T.J., 42, 43
Seagram Classics Wine Company, The, 36
Secrist, Richard, 93
Sequoia Grove, *label 54*
Shadow Brook Vineyard & Winery, *label 61*
Shafer, *label 52*
Shaw, Charles Vineyard & Winery, *label 60*, 64–65,
  67
Shrem, Jan, 82
Signorello, *label 63*
Silver Oak, *label 60*
Silverado Hill Cellars, *label 55*
Silverado Trail, 4, 65, 67, 95, 120, 141, 147, 151
Silverado Vineyards, 36, 38–39, *label 58*
Simpson, Susan, 126
Sinskey, *label 55*
Sky, *label 62*
Smith, Charles, Stuart, 110, 111
Smith, Don, 77
Smith-Madrone, *label 57*, 110, 111, 164, 165
Snowden, *label 54*
Soda Canyon Vineyards, *label 59*
Sorensen Ranch, 4
Sparkling wine, xx, 25, 36, 48, 49, 102, 103, 111,
  141, 162
Spottswoode Winery, *label 60*, 84, 85
Spring Mountain Vineyards, xii, xx, *label 63*, 162
Spring Mountain, i, vi–vii
Spring Valley, 67, 68–69, 120–121
St. Andrew's Vineyard, *label 58*
St. Clement Vineyards, x, *label 54*, 104, 105
St. Helena Star, 86–87, 89
St. Helena: i, xv, xxi, 20, 53, 67, 89, 108, 129, 132,
  149, 156; Hometown Harvest Festival, 88, 89
St. Supéry Vineyards and Winery, *label 52*, 99,
  162, 163
Stag's Leap Wine Cellars, xx, 41, *label 56*, 82
Stag's Leap xii, xxi
Staglin Family Vineyard, *label 55*
Stags' Leap, *label 57*
Star Hill, *label 61*
Steltzner, *label 60*
Sterling Vineyards, xii, xx, *label 60*, 74, 75, 149,
  159, 160–161
Stone, Michael, Ann, xx

Stonegate, *label 52*
Stonewolf, *label 58*
Stony Hill Vineyard, *label 58*, 155
Storybook Mountain Vineyards, *label 58*
Stratford, *label 58*
Straus, *label 52*
Streblow Vineyards, *label 56*
Sullivan Vineyards, *label 61*
Summit Lake Vineyards, *label 62*
Summit Winery, xviii, xix
Sunny St. Helena Winery, *label 52*
Sutter Home Winery, xix, *label 52*, 124, 125
Swanson, *label 54*

Tchelistcheff, André, 78, 79, 159
Terraces, The, *label 59*
Thomas-Hsi Vineyard, *label 62*
Three Palms Vineyard, xxi
Togni, Philip Vineyard, *label 54*
Tonnellerie Francaise-French Cooperage of
  America, 108
Traulsen Vineyards, *label 56*
Trefethen: family 25; Vineyards, *label 54*
Tudal, *label 59*
Tulocay Winery, 42, *label 63*

Upper Valley Recycling, 44–45
Upton, John, Sloan, xxi

Vaca range, xiv, xv
Vega, Carmen, 14, 16–17
Vichon, *label 57*
Villa Helena, *label 54*
Villa Mt. Eden, *label 52*
Villa Ragazzi, *label 62*
Villa Zapu, *label 58*
Vine Hill Ranch, 6–7, 8
Vose, *label 56*

Wermuth, *label 52*
White Rock Vineyards, *label 62*
White Zinfandel, 48
Whitehall Lane, *label 55*
Whitford, *label 52*
Wild hyacinths, 146, 147
Winery Lake Vineyard, 159
Winiarski, Warren, 82
Winter Creek Winery, *label 59*
Work, Henry, 108, 109

Yount, George, xv, xvii
Yountville, xv, xxi, 8, 25, 48–49, 114, 151
Yverdon, *label 59*

Zago, Juan, 118, 119
ZD, xx, *label 52*
Zinfandel, xvi, xix, xx, xxi, 71, 156

Additional photo credits

xvii: Fred Bauman, Mrs. Helen Mondavi
Ventura; xviii: Mrs.Gladys E.Wichels, Brother
Timothy Diener F.S.C.; xix: Sutter Home
Winery, Brother Timothy Diener F.S.C.; 136:
William Helsel/Abecassis Photography; 137:
Faith Echtermeyer/The Napa Valley Wine
Auction

The Grapecrusher, *a bronze sculpture by Gino Miles greets
visitors who approach Napa Valley from the south. Erected in 1987,
it is dedicated to the workers who labor in the vineyards.*

Designed by Gerard A. Valerio
Edited by Tia Hamilton O'Rear
Project Coordinated by Valerie S. Presten
Composed in Bembo by Ellen Kirby

Printed in Hong Kong by Everbest Printing Co., Ltd
through Asiaprint Ltd, Laguna Niguel, California